At the Bottom

A Woman's Life in Central America

by Luisa González

Original title: *A Ras del Suelo*

New Earth Publications
Berkeley, California

Bringing this book before the U.S. public has been a longtime labor of love by Regina Pustan, translator, Robert French, editor, and Maria Ogalde Gallardo, researcher.

Cover designed by Brook Nelson.
Woodcut by Francisco Amighetti.

For information, write to:

Regina Pustan, P.O. Box 60724, Palo Alto, CA 94306

Robert French, 83 Durfee Street, New Bedford, MA 02740

New Earth Publications
P.O. Box 4790, Berkeley, CA 94704

Library of Congress Catalog Number: 92-083796

International Standard Book Number: 0-915117-12-6

Printed in the United States of America

Table of Contents

Translator's Dedication and Acknowledgment

Dedicated with love and respect to the happy memory of Pearl Ewald, Quaker (1894-1988). Pearl's example inspired and helped many to take that decisive step from feeling and thinking to joining others in action.

Grateful thanks to Pearl's colleagues and supporters in the Women's International League for Peace and Freedom and the Southern Florida Coalition for Peace, Jobs, and Justice, especially to my old friend Rose Keenan, and to many others at home and abroad working to help the people of Central America.

Preface

I first read Luisa González' prizewinning autobiography *A Ras del Suelo* and her autobiographical play of the same title in 1984 in San José, Costa Rica. I sat in the back room of her small bookstore, situated a couple of blocks from the University of Costa Rica, behind the Cathedral of San Pedro. The store just fit into an old-fashioned one-story brick cottage with a gate and short pebbled path leading up to it. As I read her autobiography, surrounded by shelves and tables of books in many languages from all over the world, I found myself laughing, crying, or doing both at once. Her unpretentious style made me feel she was speaking directly to me. Her book gave me a remarkable zoom lens view into her life and that of her family and neighbors.

It struck me forcibly that, at all costs, Luisa González' writings must be translated so that English-speaking readers could enjoy and appreciate her and find out what life is really like in Central America for the poor—that is, for eighty-five percent of the population. In the tradition of José Martí, she has fought alongside the workers and the poor in the struggle for a better life. Her work is rare both in Central America and elsewhere in the world because it is written by an educated working-class woman. She tells about childhood experiences—of special interest because nearly half the population in Central America is fifteen years or under.

Depicted in the cover illustration of the Spanish edition of Luisa González' autobiography is an old-fashioned flatiron, the kind heated by hot coals placed inside, which her mother used for twenty years until it wore out. In the background is a woman hanging up wash, with children helping her. Luisa has acquired a unique collection of some fifty coal-heated flatirons sent to her by her readers.

While the book is an account of everyday life and events that took place in the early part of this century, the living and working conditions that Luisa describes persist today for the vast majority of Central America's people. We owe her a great debt of gratitude for opening our eyes to what life is like for most Central Americans.

Regina Pustan

Introduction

Luisa González was born on April 25, 1904 in "the most poverty-stricken, filthy, scandal-ridden and dissolute barrio in the capital of Costa Rica," her description in her famous autobiography. Despite this background but with the help of her mother and other family members, she became the first person in the history of her family to obtain the Costa Rican equivalent of a high school education. She used this step-up to work as a schoolteacher for fourteen years, trying to help the poor as she had been helped. Finally she was forced to recognize that education alone could not provide an escape and future potential for malnourished children who lacked adequate housing, health care, and family nurture.

Luisa González' personal crusade to change the social situation in which her family, her neighbors, and her pupils were trapped led her to become involved in leftist politics and to join Costa Rica's Communist party, with which she has remained closely identified. Many Latin Americans and other oppressed peoples around the world wanted to bring about fundamental social and economic change in their countries; they looked for guidance and inspiration to the Marxist-Leninist principles and strategies that helped engineer the 1917 overthrow of the czarist government of Russia. Organized in 1929, but officially founded in 1931, Costa Rica's Communist party grew in influence because of its key role in the 1934 Atlantic zone banana strike and its efforts to win social legislation. Used to describe the party before the 1948 civil war in Costa Rica, the label *communismo criollo* ("homegrown communism") encapsulated the domestic origin and orientation of the party.[1]

The Costa Rican Communist party effectively used education, in conjunction with other aspects of its political program, to give workers a voice in shaping the direction of their country. The party offered a broad variety of classes and other educational programs for workers: at the end of her autobiography, Luisa González is setting out to teach her first party-sponsored class for workers. After she was fired from her teaching job because of her political activism, she and her husband, a university professor, established a free school for workers, which offered classes on the history of Costa Rica and the history of the international workers' movement. That was only the beginning of her social and political work for her country.

A legend in her own lifetime, Luisa González has been an outspoken leader of the common people of Costa Rica as well as a celebrated writer. Known as a fiery and eloquent speaker, she has been a champion of social and economic justice, especially of the rights of women and children of the poorest worker and peasant families. She was a founder of the Costa Rica Women's Alliance, which has advocated for the rights of working women, including the traditionally powerless and neglected peasant women and urban domestic workers, and carried out solidarity efforts on behalf of women and children in Nicaragua and El Salvador.

Her commitment to social and economic justice has extended beyond the borders of her country. As she has helped launch projects to assist women and their families in other Central American countries, she has worked to oppose the dictatorial governments that are at the roots of injustice and poverty. Her support for the Sandinistas of neighboring Nicaragua dates back to 1961, when they began their struggle to overthrow the United States-backed Somoza dictatorship. After the Sandinistas' 1979 triumph, she helped to organize busloads

---

[1]A good account of the Communist party of Costa Rica is contained in John Patrick Bell, *Crisis in Costa Rica: The 1948 Revolution* (Austin: University of Texas Press, 1971).

of Costa Rican families to visit Nicaragua, thereby enabling them to see for themselves what things were actually like, in order to undercut anti-Sandinista propaganda circulated by Costa Rica's mainstream media.

For more than half a century, Luisa González has been publishing a steady stream of articles on a wide range of topics, including education, children's literature, youth, and politics. She also served for eleven years as editor and co-publisher of the children's monthly magazine *Triquetraque.*

Two chapters of Luisa González' autobiographical work in progress appeared in 1945 and 1946 in the literary review *Repertorio Americano,* published by Joaquin García Monge.[2] In the repression that followed the short, bloody 1948 civil war which reactionary forces won, police searched her home and confiscated the manuscript. It was never returned. Close to twenty years passed before she, at the urging of friends, resumed the task of writing her autobiography.

Her autobiography *A Ras del Suelo* was first published in 1970: it tells the story of her life up to 1932 when she was in her late twenties. It was an immediate success, and has been reprinted nine times and read by people of all classes. Wishing to reach more people, she turned her story into a play with the same title. Produced in 1974 by the National Company of the Theater under the direction of the now famous impresario and drama professor Luis Carlos Vasquez, the play ran for over a hundred performances. The play later toured Panama and Venezuela. It was produced in English at the Richmond Shepard Theater in Hollywood, California in Decem-

---

[2]An account of what became Chapter 7 appeared in Volume XLII, No. 7 (Saturday, November 24, 1945), pp. 106-107, while a version of Chapter 1 was published in Vol. XLII, No. 19 (Saturday, September 28, 1946), pp. 292-293.

ber 1989, under the sponsorship of Pacifica radio station KPFK-FM in Los Angeles.[3]

Luisa González received the prestigious Costa Rican Aquileo J. Echeverría award for outstanding achievement in literature in 1970 for her book and again in 1974 for her play.

Michael Gold's highly autobiographical *Jews Without Money* (1930)[4] served as a source of inspiration and a model for Luisa González: "My book is like a sister book to it," she stated.[5] Just as Gold cast his mother, whom he describes as a "brave and beautiful proletarian woman," as the "heroine" of his book, so Luisa González wrote her book to recount the story of her mother, an illiterate woman who took in washing and ironing for a living, and her mother's determined struggle to put her oldest child through school. Her expressed intent was to "exalt," or celebrate, the lives, work, and aspirations of poor women like her mother. Like Gold's fictionalized autobiography, Luisa González' book ends on a note of anticipation occasioned by her political awakening.

In a significant sense, she has never stopped teaching. As she observed,[6] "When young people, especially students and workers, read my book, they can compare their own lives with what is in the book and then they can see that it is the same life of the poor people." Her free evenings and weekends are often devoted to meetings

---

[3]English and Spanish audiotapes of Luisa González' autobiography and the radio adaptations of the play are available from Pacifica Radio Programming and Archives, 3729 Cahuenga Boulevard West, Universal City, Los Angeles, California 91604. A written text of the play, entitled *At Ground Level—Home Sweet Home in Central America* (translated by Regina Pustan, 1987), is available from Regina Pustan, P.O. Box 60724, Palo Alto, California 94306.

[4]Gold mentions in the Introduction to the 1935 edition that the book had been translated into Spanish.

[5]Telephone interview with Luisa González, July 11, 1991.

[6]Telephone interview with Luisa González, July 11, 1991.

with young people, who come to her from all over Costa Rica to hear her opinions and solicit her advice on the many problems facing youth today in Costa Rica as well as many other parts of the world—unemployment, drugs, racial discrimination, homelessness, lack of access to education and health care, and even concerning their intimate problems with family and love.

Luisa González began writing a column in 1989 for *Semanario Universidad*, the weekly newspaper of the University of Costa Rica. These articles contain fascinating vignettes of people she knew and events that she experienced. We can only hope that she continues to write about her long, active, and inspiring life.

Robert French
Maria Ogalde Gallardo

"A ras del suelo"

Xilografia de Francisco Amighetti

*I dedicate these accounts
to my mother
and to my Party.*

L.G.G.

1. The House with the Flatiron in Front

It was there, exactly there, where you could always see a black steam iron pouring smoke and red sparks into the wind—that was exactly where I lived.[1] That was my crumbling house, horribly ugly, which enclosed a world of troubles, of work, of curses and protests against "this dog's life."

I'll never forget that flatiron made of heavy cast iron, standing guard at our front door like an implacable sentinel. I'll never forget that black mouth pouring smoke forth and calling to me from the distance, "Here's where you live. This is your home, and don't you deny it. Don't be ashamed. After all, is it your fault? We're poor, very poor. That's why, whether we like it or not, we have to live in this indecent barrio."

These words rose like a curse from deep within the iron, enveloped as it was in sparks and clouds of black smoke, proclaiming to the four winds like an old gossipmonger that it was here that we lived, in this disgusting house, with its dirt floor and rickety windows.[2]

---

[1]The old-time flatiron, with hot coals inside it, was still in use in Central America in the early decades of the twentieth century. Electricity or gas are still not available in many slums and rural areas.

[2]Houses with dirt floors are still seen in Central America's rural areas and city slums.

That black flatiron lived with us for over twenty years. It was like another one of my plump, dark-skinned aunts who got started early every morning and did their jobs in the workshop, besides doing the housework and chores. The flatiron, also early in the morning, was the first to face the wind. It breathed in the fresh air to rekindle the coals inside it, after it had slept all night behind the street door of the house in the same room with us.

Yes, of course! The iron was like a member of our family, like a sister to Aunt Chana, who was always hotter than a cup without a handle, protesting and cursing her fate.

No one knew my mother's hands better than the flatiron, for my mother pushed down hard on its back for many hours day and night, pressing along the wide ironing boards over the sheets and white shirts. The wrinkles fled from their surfaces as they felt the heat pursuing them without mercy.

The black iron was also well acquainted with my aunt Carmen's large mouth, for when she blew on the coals, it was like a bellows from hell that set fire with passion to the iron's entrails. What power and energy that woman's lungs possessed! Her eyes, her nose, and her cheeks seemed about to burst, at which point she dexterously discharged exactly all the air needed to kindle the very last grains of coal into blazing flames.

They were no ordinary breaths of air that came out of my aunt Carmen's throat. With that vigor and force, it seemed as if it was her own blood circulating in red transfusion among the black coals until they came to life, and the incandescent coals sputtered forth red crystals. When triumphant blue flames, like tongues, burst from its mouth, the iron seemed to be about to speak.

The iron was never a stranger in our house. We children loved it and played with it as if it were a big sister. In its cold leisure hours, it became a locomotive that pulled trains made of empty pails and boxes. Or it would be a steamroller pressing its weight down to create beautiful streets and avenues in the make-believe cities we built in our backyard. We were all friends and family of this black iron. Even my uncles, coming home from their drinking sprees at midnight, would grab the iron by the neck and stand it at the front door, like a sentinel on duty.

We lived with that iron a good twenty years, sharing our family troubles and joys with it until one day it became deaf, deaf as my grandmother. It refused to heat up anymore and turned cold forever. Coal fires would no longer burn inside it. The iron was worn out and clogged up by all the smoke and ashes that had passed through its strong black neck. But it did not abandon its post. Now cold and stiff, it went on serving as guard at the street door, battling on alone against the wind that carried clouds of dust and trash in from the street.

There was one sure way to find our house. Everybody in the barrio explained quite clearly whenever a stranger asked for directions: "There, exactly there, where you see a black flatiron at the door, that's where the Gutiérrez family lives."

The Gutiérrez family was my mother, my aunts, my cousins, the sisters-in-law, my uncles, my grandmother, my father, and a crowd of "little ones" of all ages and sizes. All together we added up to a clan of some fifteen or twenty persons, who lived squeezed together like sardines in our shack.

Our house in that working-class barrio was an industrial and commercial center at the service of all the neighbors. Handwritten signs with bad lettering and worse spelling advertised in the only window of the house: "Shoo repairs here;" "Tortillas for sal;" "Pork tamales Saterdays;" "We do sowing," "Day borders taken." You had to make a living doing whatever jobs you could get.[3]

From the front door to the far end of the backyard, our house was an immense, strictly organized workshop, in which all the members of the family worked without pause, from my grandmother of sixty down to the smallest children able to run errands or carry firewood.

In our house, we never did have a living room or separate bedrooms as such, or a dining room or a library—nothing of the sort. Every bit of space had to be given over to the sewing machines, the ironing boards and tables, the benches and worktables of the shoe-

---

[3]High unemployment and underemployment have been a past and continuing problem in Central America.

makers, to the washtubs and water barrels, the huge cooking pots, and to an enormous brick oven with three square meters of surface area. Every day the oven would bake ten and twenty *cuartillos* of corn in cornmeal biscuits and *tamal asado*.[4] Our pieces of equipment were our means of production, and we had to grant them priority of place if we wanted to make sure of our daily bread.

For that matter, did we even own any special furniture that might occupy space in our home? No armchairs, no sofas, no wardrobes, no dressers, no desks! Nothing, nothing! Just a few old beds, some folding cots and a few large beds with sleeping mats and fiber matting. We squeezed them in between the sewing machines, next to the cobblers' benches, between the washtubs and ironing boards, or in some unused corner. Nobody lay sleepless, nobody suffered from insomnia. So we did not worry if we had to sleep on the floor or on some hard boards.

It was my job to sweep out that big workshop every morning, which was like sweeping up the market. You had to push the broom very hard to get the dirt floor cleared of the leather cuttings, fabric remnants, peelings, scraps of paper, banana leaves, splinters of wood, and all the garbage that accumulated during the day.

Out in the damp and muddy backyard, the youngsters of the neighborhood used to wait for the trash to look for scraps of patent leather, nails, and little rags to add to their playthings.

In spite of everything, in the midst of so much hustle and bustle, there was time and good humor to give free rein to singing. My seamstress aunts and my shoemaker uncles with their beautiful voices used to harmonize together on all the popular songs of the day. At the same time, they made the wheels of the sewing machines turn fast and pounded the moistened leather, their little hammers

---

[4]*Cuartillos* were containers used to measure corn, beans, etc., said to hold about eight to ten pounds of corn (telephone interview with Luisa González, August 23, 1993). *Tamal asado* is a sweet cornmeal cake. It is made of sour cream, eggs, cornmeal, cheese, and sugar. Some recipes also include raisins and cinnamon.

marking the rhythm. We youngsters accompanied the chorus on combs wrapped in tissue paper.

Our large workshop continued to operate until eleven or twelve at night, especially on Saturdays. That was the day for delivery of finished clothing and well-polished shoes, of tamale orders, and of dozens of wrapped bundles of washed and ironed laundry, spotless and without a single wrinkle.

Toward midnight, fatigue and sleep overcame all such activity. Little by little, the house fell silent. Weary, like beasts of burden, we lay down and slept deeply, on hard, filthy beds, and wrapped in torn and faded covers.

The sleepless, sharp-pointed scissors glittered coldly on the sewing machines. The knife blades shone on the cobblers' benches. The silence of the little hammers signaled the end of the working day.

Behind the street door, like a faithful watchman, the black flatiron went on with its fight against the wind, which kept trying to squeeze in through the lock and the cracks.

Like powerful motors, silent and greased, our bodies rested in a crowded heap.

In the dark, from my corner, I could see the bony backs of my uncles in their mesh undershirts, the broad hips of my aunts, and the fat arms of my grandmother, touching the children's dirty little cheeks. Under the covers and burlap sacks, the bodies seemed to take on the shapes of mountains, hills, and deep hollows, rising and falling to the rhythm of each one's breathing and the snores of my father and my grandmother.

The heavy air, pervaded by the odor of tamales, leather, smoke and sweat, inundated those narrow rooms, dark and without ventilation, suffocating me, body and soul, as an adolescent girl of thirteen.[5]

---

[5]Many of the poorest homes lack any windows or have just a cutout in a wall. At night, the opening is closed off from inside by a hinged wooden shutter folding down from the top or by a sliding wooden panel from the

Then in the darkness I went to find the black cold flatiron. I put my hands around it and pressed my burning cheeks to it, trying to cool my skin, without being able to escape from that atmosphere saturated with sweat and fleas. I closed my eyes and pressed my thirsty lips together while I recalled the song I had learned in school a few weeks before:

> "Home, sweet home
> The home of my memories
> I yearn to come back to you.
> There is no place under the sky
> Sweeter than my home.[6]"

---

side. In such homes, doors are often kept shut at night by a wooden crossbar or a heavy pole wedged against the door.

[6]A popular song in Latin America, *"Hogar de mis Recuerdos"* ("Home of My Memories") is a variation of the English song "Home, Sweet Home," written by the U.S. playwright and poet John Howard Payne (1791-1852), with music by the English composer and conductor Sir Henry Rowley Bishop (1786-1855).

2. Our Neighbors, "the Fallen Women"

In La Puebla barrio, in the vicinity of Porfirio Brenes School, there used to exist for years those little hole-in-the-wall grocery and liquor stores with names that seemed strange and mysterious to us, like "Warship of Spain", "The Doll," or "Pelayo.[1]" How and why did they ever happen to turn up in that barrio? Who can say?

What was the reason for signs like these in such a working-class barrio? Who could be the proprietors of these little businesses, the names of which appeared so oddly evocative? Perhaps the owners were from Europe and had recorded their memories and their nostalgia in these picturesque signs.

Back in the year 1912, La Puebla was the most poverty-stricken, filthy, scandal-ridden, and dissolute barrio in the capital. It was the area where vice, poverty, and prostitution flourished the most luxuriantly. There in that barrio, in the red-light district itself, was where my "home, sweet home" was located.

La Puebla owed its notoriety basically to the fact that it was in this barrio that a score or so of the poorest slum prostitutes had settled, their enterprises giving the area its crudest, most violent, and most grotesque colors.

For us youngsters, children of proletarian families, the streets and hovels where those women lived presented a daily show—

---

[1]Legendary hero (died 737), founder of the kingdom of Asturias, who defeated a Muslim expedition at Covadonga in 722, said to have initiated the end of Muslim rule over Spain.

tempting, full of mystery, and providing morbid and precocious teaching on the thorniest of sex topics. Every last one of us, curious and full of mischief, secretly harbored the most ridiculous and bizarre fantasies about the lives and wonders of the women that everyone called "women of the merry life," "prostitutes," and "whores."

We knew that the word "whore" was a dirty word and showed extremely bad manners and that we must never say it. We learned that lesson on the day that Aunt Chana rubbed a hot chili pepper over the lips of my cousin Carlos, who used to enjoy going around repeating that forbidden word.

"Women of the merry life"—why did they call them that? Of the merry life? Of what life, for heaven's sake? No, they were not merry, those women whose strange features etched themselves so deeply in my childish mind.

I can never forget those women, human beings deformed by misery and vice. Some were old and fat, others skinny and wrinkled, and their faces were daubed like masks whose horrible grimaces were reproaches to a filthy society.

How could anyone ever forget that black woman with her pouting lips, whose exuberance expressed itself in a pair of trembling buttocks that earned her the nickname of "Black Pudding"?

And how could you fail to remember the blonde with the head of hair like corn silk, the one they used to call "Poached Egg"? And what about poor Sylvia, thin and pale, assuredly tubercular? Where can she be now? Maybe she is going around begging alms, or perhaps she is already a little mound of anonymous earth in the cemetery of the poor—the Calvo.

All of us children in the barrio knew, much better than we knew our multiplication tables, the names and stories that made the rounds from mouth to mouth about the "amazing lives of the prostitutes" of La Puebla. One time we even naïvely played as prostitutes. We dressed up in our aunts' long dresses, painted our cheeks and lips, and set fire to dry leaves in imitation of the burning of incense lit by those sinners—and by virtuous ladies as well—in order to attract good male clientele.

We poor children of that slum barrio did not have at our disposal the marvelous tales of fairies, adventures and enchanted palaces by Andersen, the brothers Grimm, and Perrault. We were living in the very bowels of that monstrous world which filled our minds with morbid fantasies, formed in the seething crucible of the red-light district.

Once, egged on by mischief and curiosity, we asked our aunt Chana, "Why do they call those ladies 'prostitutes' and 'women of the merry life'?"

"Don't be such nosy busybodies! You're not old enough to know such things. Who told you to ask about things that are none of your business?" retorted Chana, giving us a shove and letting us know that such questions had to be added to the list of our sins, like the bad thoughts that we had to confess to the priest at Our Lady of Sorrows Church.

A raucous burst of laughter drowned out my aunt Chana's scolding. My shoemaker uncles at their worktables answered our question with brutal frankness: "You know why they call them 'women of the merry life'? Why, simply because they're just bums, because they don't have to work to make a living. They're shameless. They lay around loafing all day long, while we here are sweating our heads off."

Jokes and coarse and vulgar remarks followed the family discussion until my mother, infuriated, imposed silence in an attempt at consideration for the children's innocence. We youngsters listened, puzzled by the condemnation and scorn men always express when they talk about these poor creatures.

"Shut up! Keep still, for the love of God!" said my mother. "Don't talk so dirty in front of the children. Remember, we have three girls growing up in the family. God can punish us!"

"What shameless bandits men are! They go and have themselves a good time with these poor women. Then afterwards they eat them up alive, heap scorn on them, and make fun of them, telling jokes and making disgusting remarks about them without limit," was my aunt Carmen's retort, and she worked the bellows as if it was hell itself that ought to swallow up so much infamy and blasphemy.

"How strange!" I thought to myself. "My mother and Aunt Carmen seem to be defending the prostitutes. How can that be?" There in the depths of my heart I felt, with a strange feeling of fear, that we children also had a certain sympathy, dominated perhaps by curiosity and mystery, for these sinful neighbors who added such a picturesque note to the barrio.

How could we help admiring them? Weren't they the ones who hurried to help us—like the Samaritan women—when the earthquake struck in Cartago on the tragic night of May 4, 1910?[2] They carried big pitchers of water to give all the women and children—we were choking from the clouds of dust falling from the adobe walls. "How brave and generous," we thought.

Nobody had the slightest hesitation about drinking big gulps of the water these women offered. They were not afraid, had no thought of saving themselves, did not devote themselves to reciting the Trisagion,[3] but came to help and protect the children, the women, and the old people. At that very time, we were studying Sacred History to make our First Communion. We saw the prostitutes as the true embodiment of the pious women. And for years and years in our family, they retold the beautiful story of these sinful women, a story that left us children in amazement.

Experience and daily life in the barrio served to confirm us in our secret sympathy for the prostitutes.

They were the ones who many a time saved us from a whipping for having lost a ten centimos or a peseta coin of the change from the grocery store. Many times we saw them open their perfumed purses to give us the coins we had lost or secretly filched to buy little flasks of sugared liqueur.

These women seemed to us to be true guardian angels when they quickly rescued us from punishment at home and when they affectionately treated us for a scrape on the knee which gave us trouble walking.

---

[2]Born on April 25, 1904, Luisa was six years of age in 1910.

[3]A prayer to the Holy Trinity used in special circumstances.

Our secret sympathy for them grew, but we hid it because of the terror we felt deep in our hearts. We knew it was a sin to have anything to do with these women. We were filled with horror, feeling ourselves already on the road to hell, pushed along by those sinful hands.

Our moral concepts, barely into the formative stages, twisted in strange confusion. Still children, we could not understand or explain to ourselves why and how such women, as people said, were the shame and disgrace of La Puebla barrio.

Many times we shed tears when we saw the ambulance loading up poor Sylvia. Drunk and haggard, she would be saying good-by to her little gray-brown cat, left meowing at the rickety door of her shack.

My aunt Chana boxed our ears to keep us from watching the degrading spectacle and, with a catch in her voice, would say to us: "Why, you silly kids! What is there to cry about? Can't you see Sylvia is drunk and the police have to obey the law?"

She was putting on an act. But we could tell she had a lump in her throat—her voice had a tremor to it.

We would explain to her that it was not for Sylvia that we were crying, but for the poor kitten, meowing in a voice that grated like a rusty hinge. Then my aunt Chana fixed a milk soup in a small bowl and ordered us to take it to the poor animal. In joy and triumph, we went and carried out this satisfying task during the time Sylvia was in the "Cotton Gin.[4]"

We were like all children everywhere in the world—good little youngsters, sentimental, generous, and grateful. We grew up in that sordid, miserable barrio like so many plants growing through dry, hard dirt. But in our souls flourished the virtues that my mother and my aunts, by hook or by crook, cultivated in us with energy and singular grace in that home in the barrio of La Puebla.

---

[4]Prostitutes taken into custody were brought to the convent of the Bethlehemite order of nuns, who operated a cotton gin which the prostitutes worked during their jail sentence.

*

One fine day a case of conscience occurred that caused a huge and violent upheaval in the bosom of our family. Was it perhaps a matter of philosophy, politics, or religion? Not at all. It was something more complex. The question was whether we could or could not sell to those sinful ladies the goods and services we produced in our incipient cottage industry, which provided the family livelihood.

The temptation was very great. Scruples of conscience bowed before the opportunity to get such good customers in the neighborhood. They did not haggle over prices. What was more, they paid cash on the barrel.

Maybe it was the devil who directed the leader of that band of "pale birds" toward the door of our house. Everyone called her "Polly" because of the gaudy parrot-like colors of her provocative attire, which served to advertise from a distance her illicit profession and her plentiful earnings from it.

Well, the aforesaid Polly came bringing Uncle Daniel a pair of white slippers, so he could put taps on the heels. Flirting and joking with him, she gave him the job. Of course, my uncle, being quick on the uptake, offered to personally deliver the slippers to her house that very evening.

Poor Polly had not gone ten steps from our house when a storm of protests and reproaches broke out against that bold woman who had the nerve to come and tempt the men of this hardworking family. "That hussy! For shame! How dare you have any dealings with that indecent tramp!" cried my aunt Lola. She was a confirmed spinster, impeccably attired in a nun's habit of Our Lady of Mount Carmel.[5] Lola claimed it gave her the privilege and authority to judge left and right, separating the righteous from the sinners. With fury indescribable, as if she were the archangel St. Michael casting

---

[5]In their account of social life and custom in Costa Rica (*Costa Rican Life*, New York: Columbia University Press, 1944), John and Mavis Biesanz note: "Religious habits are still worn by hundreds of lay women and girls, but are not as common as formerly. 'This is as a promise or penance to secure some favor or good,' writes a student, 'such as a physical cure.'"

Adam and Eve forth from Paradise, she grabbed the pair of slippers, the corpus delicti, and threw them out in the middle of the street, attempting thus to rescue the honor of our house.

I can still see the pair of white slippers swimming in the mud of the street, like little ducklings, with their feathers plucked by the virtuous hands of that intransigent old maid.

In three bounds, my infuriated uncle leaped into the street and recovered the pair of slippers. With cruel vengeance, he rubbed and scrubbed them clean on the Carmelite skirts of my aunt Lola, in an effort to tarnish her saintliness with the human sins of poor Polly.

"By all that's holy," my uncle shouted, "we're going to get this matter cleared up once and for all. Can we do business with these women, yes or no? Is their money worth any less than Doña Lupita's or Doña Lucrecia's?"

"It's not the same thing. Don't make such vulgar comparisons," said my aunt Carmen. "You know very well that this money comes from evil, that it is dirty money, very dirty, that it can bring evil spells and curses upon us."

"And do you suppose," retorted my uncle, "that the money we get from the old women comes perfumed and washed in holy water? Don't make me laugh! Who doesn't know where those crisp new bills come from or those checks signed with flourishes? They're like magic wands and produce the most disgusting and scandalous business deals. Do you want to tell me that that money isn't dirty and evil? Do you think if money comes out of a fancy leather checkbook that makes it holy and blessed?"

"Son of God!" cried out my aunt Chana, bewildered and frightened. "Where do you get such strange ideas? According to you, all the money in the world is dirty and evil, even the money in the collection boxes of the church!"

"Yes, ma'am, even that money is dirty if it comes from the wallets of rogues and thieves," declared my uncle.

Poor Aunt Lola could not stand it any longer. She flung herself at my uncle Daniel, shaking him by the shoulders and uttering gross insults: "Blasphemer! Foulmouthed! Freemason! Atheist!"

This hubbub paralyzed all the family's activities. The matter involved a moral problem of the first magnitude, complicated like everything in our society by the damned money. We had to have money every day, like air, just to stay alive.

All the family members threw themselves with passion into the discussion. My grandmother forgot the tortillas and let them burn on their earthenware hearth. The milk boiled over. The iron, scorching Dr. Esquivel's shirt, gave the alarm with clouds of black smoke and halted the discussion on the spot.

Following the noisy discussion came the logical and practical conclusions imposed on us by life's realities. The "moral" to be drawn was clear: outside of poor Lola, all the members of the family came to accept the truth of the blunt and realistic arguments put forth by Uncle Daniel.

The "moral" problem, hotly discussed by the whole family, came to be perfectly clearly defined in conformity with reality. We could sell our tortillas of crushed corn to the poor prostitute Sylvia as well as to Doña Elisa, the teacher living next door to the Modern Theater.

We could sew dresses for Doña Lucrecia the same as we could for Polly, and we could do the laundry for Doña Lupita as well as for "Poached Egg."

Underneath the shoemaker's bench, the pairs of shoes belonging to the honorable Daughters of Mary[6] lay jumbled together in strange and ridiculous fraternity with those of the fallen women. What a tangled up world this is!

As for us children, we were sent impartially to deliver finished work to Pacific barrio, to the barrio of Our Lady of Sorrows Church, or to the hovels where the women of the merry life lived.

My poor aunt Lola could no longer bear the "immorality" of the family, which, according to her religious precepts, had fallen very low into a most horrible abyss of sin and cynicism.

One day the poor woman packed her few rags into a coarse cotton sack and left to go to work as family washerwoman in the home of Doña Lucrecia. Aunt Lola naïvely believed that in this illus-

---

[6]A lay organization of women active in support of the Roman Catholic Church.

trious house, virtue and religious zeal shown everywhere, like stars in the sky. To judge by the bright shine of the floors, by the beautiful rugs and the sweet-smelling flowers in the garden surrounding the mansion, it had to be supposed that virtue and honor went hand in hand in such lordly surroundings.

Poor Lola was mistaken. Less than a year had passed when there was a knock at the door of our house, and she came in, pale and haggard. The blotches on her face and on her prominent cheekbones betrayed her five months' pregnancy. Doña Lucrecia's husband, a Knight of the Society of Mary,[7] who owned a handsome checkbook with his name engraved in gold, showed no respect for the nun's habit of Our Lady of Mount Carmel. And so, just like that, he made the house laundress pregnant. Our little first cousin, taken into our home, grew up together with us. Along with us, he went running errands up and down the streets, bringing in cartloads of firewood, carrying water, and at the same time learning the harsh and cruel lessons that life gives to all the children that live and grow in the slum outskirts of the cities.

---

[7]A Roman Catholic organization formed for the purposes of providing for devotion to the Virgin Mary, for religious education, and for other church activities.

3.   A Strange Adventure

> It's true—it's no fairy tale
> There is a Guardian Angel
> Who takes you and carries you like the wind
> And goes with children wherever they go.
>
> — Gabriela Mistral[1]

In our house, as in so many other houses rich or poor, we too had a vulgar and horrible color print hanging on the wall from a crooked, rusty nail. The picture showed the Guardian Angel lovingly spreading his white wings over a pair of fat, pink children who were running across a bridge. They were chasing blue butterflies along a path strewn with fragrant lilies and roses.

For us, that angel always remained painted on the wall. What would have become of his dazzling purity if he had ever dared to walk behind us, watching over us along those alleys and filthy, dark streets, saturated with sin and misery? That unlucky angel would have had to roll his celestial vestments up to his knees and even leave his immaculate wings hanging from a nail, because—good

---

[1]Gabriela Mistral (1889-1957), Chilean poet and educator. She was the first woman poet as well as the first Latin American to win the Nobel Prize (1945). The epigraph is from *"El Angel Guardián"* ("The Guardian Angel"), which was included in Mistral's first book of poetry, *Desolación (Desolation)*.

Lord!—those are rough paths that misery treads in these slum barrios.

Fortunately, it had never occurred to this good angel to undertake such a dangerous adventure. What would have become of him and his celestial purity if he had made so bold as to carry out his duty to take care of these urchins? They were badly behaved ragamuffins who had long since lost their last shreds of innocence, caught in the web of vice and misery. Lord, no! Our angel stayed very haughty, blind, impassive, and nailed to the wall, showing off his purity as if it were an advertisement for cotton candy.

To tell the truth, from our earliest years we had to learn to handle alone the blows life rained on us left and right, as we ran hither and thither earning our daily bread any way we could. We couldn't be choosy. We had no idea whether or not we had any guardian angel in back watching over us. We never felt any protection nor any divine tenderness from these winged beings. Like the one in that picture, they take care of the children who are rosy pink and favored by fortune.

Several years later, when I began to have my doubts about matters of faith, I asked myself with distrust and timidity, "Would that guardian angel have accompanied us on our deliveries to the houses of the women of the merry life? Why didn't that angel ever help us by lightening the load of those heavy baskets and sacks full of tamales and tortillas that we had to deliver all over the barrio?" No, no! His wings of delicate white foam could barely withstand the perfumed breezes from the woods and gardens. As a girl of ten, my skinny arms were stronger than those thick, curled, stiff, motionless, cold wings.

When I recall some of those crude, bizarre adventures we innocent children lived through, I almost feel sorry for that poor defenseless angel, whose winged purity would not let him walk on earth. We children and youth of La Puebla knew how to get around in this "vale of tears" better than he did.

It so happened one day, when we were delivering a bundle of washed and ironed laundry to the prostitute Fat Lips' shack, that she called my cousin Julio aside. With an air of great mystery, she made him the following proposition:

"Look, sonny, I need a boy like you, somewhere between thirteen and fifteen, to come Friday and put out burning incense for me. You know I pay good money. It won't do you any harm. It's just that for such things a boy like you is needed, that's all. Don't get scared. Nothing is going to happen to you. Come between dark and daylight, around six-thirty in the evening."

I was waiting for Julio on the sidewalk across the street. When he came back, his ears were red, he was biting his nails, and he pushed me toward the nearest doorway. "What happened? What did that prostitute say to you?" I asked with mischievous concern.

"How should I know.... Imagine, she wants me to come Friday and blow out some burning incense that they have. She offered me five colons and some other things besides.[2]"

"So what? Are you afraid to go? If you don't want to go, I'll go," I said, putting on a bold, brave front. At the same time, I was dying of curiosity and mischievousness.

"Don't be an idiot! Where'd you get that idea? If your mama hears that, she'll give you a good licking. You know we're forbidden to go inside those houses."

"But why can't I go?"

"Quit making a pest of yourself! Fat Lips says it has to be a boy like me. Little girls are no use for that," replied my cousin boastfully. Leaving me behind, he loaded a sack of corn on his shoulders and walked on ahead, acting like a big man.

Only the two of us were in on this strange and dangerous matter, and we knew it had to be kept in strictest secrecy. Thus, when we got home, without any previous arrangement we uttered not a single word, did not open our lips, and kept everything under wraps with only meaningful glances.

Ten thousand times we had been told never to dare to go inside any of the shacks where those women lived and never to accept even one piece of candy from their hands. Nothing from them! Absolutely nothing! We could only receive payment for the sewing, for the clean

---

[2]Established in 1896 as the monetary unit of Costa Rica, the colon is divided into 100 centimos.

laundry, and for the tortillas. That could not be helped if we wanted to earn a little money from them. "Anyone of you ever takes a step inside one of those doors, I'm giving you a good beating," my mother had said. She was always worried about the business relations we had to maintain with these women, so undesirable as neighbors but such generous, good-paying customers.

Fat Lips' proposition kept making us choke as we ate our food. Timidly we kept glancing, trying to keep my mother and my aunts from finding out about the mess that we were about to get ourselves into.

"These kids are acting like worms, they can't stay still. They must have something up their sleeves," said my aunt Carmen, at the same time ordering us to go and bring in a cartload of firewood that had just been dumped in front.

Very obediently and submissively, we left at once to carry out her orders, trying to hide the worries we had in our hearts.

Twilight found Julio and me climbing to the top of the pile of firewood that we had put into the big, open shed at the back of the courtyard. Way on top and speaking in low voices, we made our plans, weighing scruples of conscience and finally deciding to accept the mysterious proposal. We would go the coming Friday and carry out this strange mission.

My cousin had already heard some stories about the burning of incense. He had earned a few coins several times by buying the prostitutes small packets of the seven kinds of incense (officinal storax, copal, myrrh, etc., etc.) at Our Lady of Sorrows Pharmacy. He had only carried out errands of that sort, that was all. He had never entered any of those houses and had never taken part in any of their witchcraft.

"I swear it," he told me, trembling with fear, afraid that I might snitch on him.

All the youngsters of the barrio were well aware of the strange customs practiced by the ladies of the merry life. How could anyone help but know? Every Tuesday and Friday, the street was inundated with great waves of smoke, saturated with the smell of the seven kinds of incense that were being burned in small tin saucers and decorated bowls.

Everyone knew that such witchcraft was for the purpose of attracting male clientele to the street of sin. Of course, no one raised any fuss about that. It was quite natural. It was a kind of advertisement for the merchandise, just like for any other.

Fairies, gnomes, elves, and even the stories from *The Thousand and One Nights* found no place in the barrio of La Puebla. Our childish imaginations were fed by the stories and tales we heard told with great wealth of detail at the evening get-togethers of neighbors and family members in the workshop of the shoemakers and seamstresses.

Besides these evening parties, there were also the morning groups, made up of the neighbors in their backyards while they were hanging the wash up to dry on the wires. All these events provided crude and grotesque lessons that left us open-mouthed, with our minds in turmoil, and which put our nerves and our childish imaginations under morbid tension.

The gossip, the stories, and even the most absurd tales were an indispensable part of the day and the daily program of that crowd of women, children, men, and young people, all of us living and pushing one another aside to be able to exist.

Most of the neighbors were experts and erudite on the subject of stories, legends, superstitions, and effective magic to settle the complicated problems of love. In the slum barrios, these problems are made worse by the tragedies of poverty and ignorance, while in the residential barrios, vice and immorality are cloaked in glittering elegance and refinement.

With dignity and authority, the honorable ladies of the barrio exchanged recipes, prayers, and superstitions, as well as love potions, which they always kept on hand to cure whatever signs of waywardness their husbands might begin to show.

Doña Dorila, the old woman who dealt the cards out impartially to pious and sinner alike, was the most authoritative personage at such get-togethers. Her hoarse voice issued from between a pair of fleshy and mustachioed lips, allowing a view of several teeth framed in gold like those of a boss man. She was a remarkable expert. When she took the floor, she impressed by her picturesque repertoire of stories and legends, which she related with grace and conviction.

I remember she even kept a notebook, just like a consultant. In it she had recorded recipes for potions, rites, popular beliefs, explanations of dreams, lists of aphrodisiacs, prayers, etc., etc. That notebook, covered with blue and gold cloth, was the great repository of her rich experience, and it brought her plenty of colons every month.

She was no fool. She had found this rich vein for making money and she quickly freed herself from the flatiron and washboard, over which so many poor women of the city have to sweat.

Doña Dorila's recipes and advice never failed. That was why she had won the trust and affection of so many women, both the respectable ones and the sinners. She served all without discrimination, aside from the slight difference that on Tuesdays she received the respectable ladies—those who were married, the widows, and the virtuous spinsters. And on Fridays she devoted herself body and soul to the poor "pale birds."

In the little money sack that she kept in her exuberant bosom, the bright coins paid her by clients of the one or the other group all came together.

My uncles, vulgar and dirty talkers, gave Doña Dorila the nickname of "Three in One," referring to the bag that fitted in so well between her two breasts. Her believing and generous heart led her to donate many colons to the altar of Our Lady of Sorrows Church. Many of the barrio's little children made their First Communion because Doña Dorila had bought them their outfit and shoes for such a great event. The old lady was not stingy, that had to be granted her. She was splendid and generous with all the families of this barrio, which had raised her to such supreme heights of success and prosperity in her enterprise.

Saints and novenas, mixed in with witchcraft and recipes for potions, completed the baggage of her profession. Everybody's favorite, however, was the prayer to St. Martha. It was bought just the same by sinful women as by respectable ladies, because for miracles of love, whether legal or clandestine, there was nothing like this prayer, the text of which follows:

"St. Martha, just as you entered into Mount Galilee, enter where the lord of my heart is with that snake. You sent him to her with holy water and a hyssop. You tied her and took her with your sacred hand. Bind me to my companion, and make him mild and humble as a lamb under the sole of St. Martha Florida.

"I offer you this prayer in the name of the three nails—strong, strong, strong. I divide your heart and drink your blood. With the cord and standard, St. James arises and tells his disciples that any person who recites this prayer will humble any man and put him under the soles of the feet of St. Martha Florida. Three creeds and the votive candle."

My aunt Carmen, impassioned and combative, denied St. Martha's miracles and put all her faith in the prayer to St. Helen of the Cross. She pulled a carefully folded little paper out of her bosom and surprised the audience by declaiming the complete text of the only prayer capable of performing genuine miracles in the arts of love. In fact, the part about the three nails, in the way it is given in this prayer, was a crushing argument. How could you help but be filled with faith on hearing these sentences spoken by my aunt in a dramatic tone of desperation:

"You were and are a saint. When they crucified Christ Our Lord, you removed the three nails. One you threw in the sea, and the other you consecrated to your brother, the Emperor of the Battles. The third nail you kept yourself. Let me have that one. I don't ask you to give it to me, only lend it to me, so I can nail it...whether he is absent or present, so that he will have no pleasure or rest, neither with men nor with women, so that he will think of me first and moan and weep."

"Have patience, señora,
And place your trust in me.
She who avails herself of Helen
Will sooner or later attain her desire."

Face to face, St. Martha and St. Helen of the Cross entered into enormous competition. The get-together split into two groups of ladies with opposite opinions. Doubts were even expressed regarding St. Martha's saintliness, because it was her picture, painted in bright colors, that had won out in the houses of the prostitutes.

When the argument came to this most critical point, Doña Dorila's authoritative voice broke in with the verdict:

"Neither male nor female saints may be placed in competition. That is a mortal sin. What I advise is to recite both prayers. If one does not bring results, the other one will come through and clinch the case."

And the clever old woman did good business selling the prayers and pictures of both St. Helen and St. Martha, doubling her sales. She bought such items very cheaply in the stationery stores and sold them for twice the price. As she explained, the priest of Our Lady of Sorrows Church had blessed them, and, of course, holy water is very expensive.

"If you want to be able to lead your man around by the nose," remarked Doña Talía, "there's nothing like wrapping his picture in a piece of his old underwear and putting it under your pillow. That man will come back to you a saint. For him, there will never be another woman, only his wife. He'll never look at another 'skirt' again. He'll be faithful to you till the end of his days."

"For my part, there is nothing better than a candle cut in three," spoke up Doña Raquel, trying to top Doña Talía's advice. "You cut a candle in three pieces. On each piece, you write the name of your wayward man and the name of your rival. For the next seven days, you keep your husband's picture turned away from you. When the last bit of candle has burned down, and the candle drippings melt, you'll see an image of his beloved forming. That means that the spell has gone from the body and soul of that poor bewitched man."

All the women assented in deep faith and admiration, for every recipe gave them new weapons and means of making sure of their husband's love.

"And what about the holy water with the seven herbs?" put in Elena, my aunt by marriage. She was trying to impress her example on everyone as the only woman whose husband had never cheated on her, thanks to her sprinkling their bed every morning with some drops of this potion.

We children, who were listening on the other side of the partition, would fall asleep to the jokes and coarse bursts of laughter from my uncles. They were ridiculing these naïve and credulous señoras, so passionately defending their right to love as the most basic of all their rights.

Oh, those get-togethers around the table, where working women talk about the complicated problems of love! If only someone could have recorded on audiotape those picturesque stories, told with the healthy and clean intention of striving to win the heart of the man you are desperately in love with!

Incomparable and ingenuous tales of these women of my barrio! I'll never forget the depth of emotion in those lustrous eyes, the vigor of their gestures, and the passion of their voices, claiming the caresses and protection of the beloved man, the one who gives us children, security, sorrow, and joy.

Excited and timid, we youngsters made our comments next day in secret about the stories we had heard told at these evening get-togethers.

"What was that about leading a man by the nose?" I asked my cousin Julio. "What's the idea of doing that?"

He gave no explanation, jabbed me with his elbow, blamed me for not knowing, and called me a faultfinder, a tattletale, and bigmouthed.

*

Finally Friday arrived, the day of the great adventure. With supreme diligence and discretion, we finished all the chores that we were supposed to, in order to gain the confidence of our family members.

At six p.m. sharp, my cousin took off in a hurry to fulfill his mission at Fat Lips' place. I was left on pins and needles, imagining strange fantasies and trembling with fear and curiosity. I looked again at the picture of the Guardian Angel. He looked back at me impassively, and I understood quite clearly that he was living in the clouds, far removed from our adventures and forays.

Over an hour had passed and Julio was not back. Sitting in a corner of the front doorway at my house, I imagined macabre scenes and felt myself to be an accomplice of that dangerous mission. Could Julio have been suffocated by breathing those diabolical fumes? Could he have tripped over the brazier that burned those resins, enveloping them in blue and green clouds of smoke? Good heavens! What could be happening inside there in that prostitute's house? Why wasn't my cousin back?

I could not stand the anxiety and anguish any more. In desperation I went and shouted out at Fat Lips' place:

"Julio! Julio! What's happening? Why don't you come out? Come right out if you don't want me to tell on you."

The strong odor of the burning incense and the smoke swallowed up my shouting. The door opened part way, enough for me to see the face of the prostitute.

"Don't cry, little child of God," she said. "Why are you screaming like that? Go home, stop worrying. I'll send Julio back right away. Take these candies to eat on your way home."

Confused and trembling with fear, I went home directly to the outdoor toilet, where I could hide myself and conceal my emotions. Heeding my mother's orders, I threw the bag full of delicious cream candies into the black hole. I got on my knees on the dirty, broken boards in that toilet and began to pray to the Lonely Spirit, for I felt myself to be condemned and damned to the deepest pit in purgatory as an accomplice of such an adventure. My mother's calling and looking everywhere for me broke into the fervor of my prayers.

"To blazes with that girl! Where have you gotten yourself to? Did you forget you have to go and deliver the sewing to La Chola? You lazy girl, get going out of here fast!"

The errand came just in time to be my salvation. I had not gone two blocks when I met Julio. I did not understand why he was so startled to see me. He squeezed my arms very hard and without further ado threatened me, saying: "God help you if you say a word about this, because I'll give you a good beating. Here, you have four coins for yourself and these candies and caramels. Get away from here quick. I have to go get two packs of cigarettes for Fat Lips."

When I got back to the house, I hid the candies under my pillow. On Sunday, I put all four coins in the collection box for the Lonely Spirit for helping me to keep the secret.

Julio maintained an inexplicable and hermetic silence for all time. I was never able to get him to tell me one word about that dangerous and strange adventure.

4. Another Baby Brother

One fine day he was born, like so many others.
It was not his own decision and there was no rejoicing.
Perhaps he heard someone say that his arrival
Was damned well not needed.
But he was born—it could not be helped.

— Angela Figuera[1]

Mariana, the old midwife of the barrio, always haggard-looking, with circles under her eyes from lack of sleep, and wrapped from head to foot in a black shawl, entered silently, smoking a cigarette and carrying half a bottle of liquor and a quart of molasses in a mesh string bag. She lit a candle in my mother's room and at top speed began to recite the prayer to St. Raymund the Unborn:

"Oh, St. Raymund, never born prodigy, I come to you because of your great compassion toward your followers. Señor, special patron of pregnant women! Here I am, my saint, one of those who place themselves humbly under your protection and shelter. Saint and my defender, I humbly beg you to deliver to my Lord God the baby who is locked in the dark prison of my entrails—may it stay alive and well. Help me out of my plight so I can offer a new servant at the feet of the Lord.

---

[1]Angela Figuera Aymerich (b. 1902), Spanish poet.

Kyrie eleyson. Christe eleyson. Pater de Coelis Deus, miserere nobis...."

In the midst of the smoke and noisy commotion in our house, at that moment the Latinized phrases she recited so dramatically transformed the untrained midwife into the principal, respected, and highly skilled director of the entire process of the birth of the new being.

My grandmother blew onto the burning wood to heat the big pots of hot water faster. Meantime, my aunts shooed all the youngsters away. The children were curious and wanted to know what was happening on the other side of the kitchen partition. My aunt Chana gave out cookies, a little bag of peanuts, and some bean cakes, so that we could enjoy ourselves eating under the custard apple tree. It looked so cool and fresh at the far end of the backyard.

In low voices, timidly and with mischievous curiosity—brothers, sisters, and cousins together—we commented excitedly on the great mystery of human procreation. It was enveloped in myths and absurd legends, which at that time were falsely claimed to protect the childish innocence of the children of that period.

As a matter of fact, we older children no longer believed in those fairy tales. Like experts, we explained to the younger children the entire natural process of human sexual relations. We had received so many grotesque lessons in that barrio of La Puebla and in our own home that not a shred of naïveté or mystery was left about such matters. In the slum barrios, these are an everyday part of life, like the air we breathe.

After a long five hours of waiting, the tension was broken by the shrill cry of the newborn, informing us it had now arrived in this vale of tears. All the women began to recite the prayer to St. Raymund the Unborn in chorus. They gave infinite thanks to the Lord for the arrival of this little one, who had come to add to the endless series of children in our family, faithfully complying with the biblical command "Be fruitful and multiply."

"Now you have another little brother!" called my father from the kitchen entrance, on that rainy late afternoon in October, while he helped my grandmother get two pails and a basin full of dirty linen and bloody water out of the room.[2]

"Listen, it's another little brother for you," repeated my father more insistently.

I was holed up in the backyard shed, trying to flee from reality, for this baby was the fifth little brother who had come to squeeze our shaky family economy still further.

Had they perhaps prepared anything for his arrival? They would put him to bed in a box or even there in my mother's bed. He would be wrapped in pieces of old rags or remnants from coarse cotton sacks, and that would be all. For him there would be no cozy, warm cradle where his tender little body could cuddle up. He had not come into this world to sleep on a feather bed. He was destined for the fate of poor children.

Aunt Chana hid the dirty linen under the water trough and sprinkled the bloody water over the clumps of hollyhock, chamomile, and mint to make them bloom in all their glory. Meantime, my father was digging a hole in a corner of the yard to bury the newborn baby's afterbirth.

"Don't bury the cord," called my grandmother from the small window in the kitchen. "Put it in this little box and take it to Puntarenas to throw into the ocean. That will bring him good luck and this little fellow will never die by drowning."

"That's just a lot of foolishness," said Uncle Daniel. "How many cords have you already saved up with this little story that you're going to throw them in the sea? Have you ever gotten even as far as Virilla? Don't bother me with your fairy tales!"

Legends and superstitions of every kind and fantasies without number have arisen around this little bit of tissue that leaves such a singular and interesting scar on the belly of every mortal.

---

[2]Costa Rica's mountainous San José and surrounding areas, where over two-thirds of the country's population live, receive about 70 inches of rainfall annually, mostly during May-November.

According to the women, it has miraculous powers, like being the thread of life which ties on here, assuring the biological independence of the new being.

Wrapped in cotton like a religious medal, it should be carried by men going on a long journey, especially sailors and fishermen. It is an indispensable amulet for saving lives in the adventures and perils of the sea.

When the cord is kept in alcohol, it is a magnificent relic with great miraculous powers to drive away the evil spells and deceptions that hover like bats over the houses of the poor.

"Don't be stupid," said my uncle. "Sell it to old Dorila. She'll know how to squeeze the juice out of that confounded little piece of insides."

"Are you out of your mind? How could you even think of such an awful idea?" asked my aunt Carmen, frightened by the boldness and audacity of that unbelieving, cynical shoemaker.

Mariana, the old midwife, who was in the kitchen stuffing herself with a delicious lunch, broke into the discussion.

"These are sacred matters. They have their mysteries that Christians know nothing about. That's why we have to respect them until the day of the Last Judgment. It would be blasphemy to accept even five centimos. That could cause a curse to fall on us. My advice is to give it to Doña Dorila for a present. She is a benefactor of this barrio—it couldn't fall into better hands. She understands these mysteries to perfection and knows how to use them just right for every case and occasion. Maybe you yourself will benefit from that some day—you never know how the world turns!"

All assented in silence, obedient to the respected advice from the midwife. She was not slow on the uptake and immediately offered to bring that little bit of tissue to old Dorila, a confederate and colleague of hers in these ministrations at such high level in the life of the working-class barrios.

A crowd of dirty, bleary-eyed youngsters invaded my mother's bed to see the little "angel head" cuddled in her arms. Now smiling and calm, she asked us what name we should give the new baby.

I bit my lips and, with deep feelings of remorse, secretly repudiated my egotistical and miserly attitude. As the eldest sister, I accepted the new burden that God had laid on us—more privation, more work, and more worries. Although my father always repeated the well-worn phrase that God would provide, each time a child was born in the family, I distrusted that remark a thousand and one times. That was because I knew and felt that it did not matter to God so much as a cumin seed's worth that in our house there would not be enough bread or milk for all. I knew that another mouth meant new restrictions, a smaller share, a rationing forced on us by the increase in the number of family members.

The drippings from the candles burning to St. Raymund the Unborn ran slowly down the candlesticks. The youngsters hurried to catch them, even though the wax was still hot, so they could make little wax figures. Meantime, the littlest ones sucked on the sly on the bottle of molasses. The midwife had left it on a box for my mother to take, mixed with spoonfuls of liquor, to clean out her stomach, which had gotten rough treatment during the delivery.

In the hot, smoky kitchen, my aunts and my grandmother were hurrying to make coffee and to pat tortillas, which they baked on the brazier. In the midst of the great din, they made a thousand plans for the new baby's baptismal day. This event was perhaps the only family fiesta that reunited the relatives and closest neighbors once a year around a pot of rice pudding, along with bottles of delicious eggnog that my grandmother made, and with batter bread and squash turnovers.

"It'll have to be this coming month at the latest," called my aunt Chana from the backyard, where she was wringing out an enormous blanket, from which soapy water was streaming down into her clogs. "It can't be delayed. If—God forbid—the little boy gets sick and dies before he's baptized, he'll go straight to limbo."

"What is this nonsense? What are you talking about?" interrupted my uncle, always unbelieving and ridiculing.

"Come on now, Daniel! Don't you know that unbaptized babies die in mortal sin and fall under an eternal curse?"

"What is this stupidity? You'll have to explain that. I can't understand how you can put a newborn baby under a curse, just like that," retorted my uncle, intrigued by these stories from Aunt Chana.

"Why yes, sir. Even though you may not believe it, you ought to know that all babies who die without being baptized are condemned for all eternity. They have to suck on the tree with the bitter tits that grows in the accursed forests of limbo." From their descriptions, my aunts imagined this kind of tree to look something like the cacao shrub, whose oval fruits seem to be stuck onto the trunk and to look like turgid, full breasts ready to slake the thirst of the poor children who have never received the miraculous and blessed water of baptism. According to Christians, baptismal water has the marvelous power of washing away the stain of original sin.

"Gwamma, gwamma, what is original sin?" asked my little cousin Carlos worriedly.

"Well, child, that's the apple of Paradise that Eve gave to Adam."

"But what was wrong with the apple? Why was it a sin to eat it?" persisted little Carlos.

"Throw that boy out of this kitchen! What is he butting in here for, hanging around behind the women's skirts? Cut out all those nosy questions! The time will come when you'll be fed up and get indigestion from that kind of apple," Daniel growled in a menacing tone.

That intrigued Carlos, and he brought the matter up when the crowd of kids in the barrio got together. There he received the most grotesque and vulgar answers to his questions.

From that day on, the center of our attention became that picturesque and amusing drawing representing Paradise on Earth, with its leafy tree full of tempting red apples. There was that rogue of a snake, wicked and clever, egging poor Adam on. Holding hands with Eve and covering himself with a fig leaf, Adam was leaving Paradise, being driven out by the archangel St. Michael.

5. A Coach Ride

At the beginning of this century, the coach was the vehicle in common use. It could be seen in huge numbers everywhere on the cobblestoned streets of the capital.

This black carriage with its four wheels, drawn by a pair of handsomely decorated horses, provided all the youngsters with a daily and inexhaustible source of entertainment. The driver sat very proudly on the coachman's box outside the hood, holding the reins with elegance and style and cracking his whip over the backs of the horses.

We children found it all so exciting and thrilling. We sat in the open doorway or along the sidewalk curb, with eyes wide and mouths open, gazing at the whinnying horses, their hoofs striking sparks on the cobblestones. Then, like an expert animal trainer, the coachman would lash out with his shiny black whip and the carriage would be underway.

I'll never forget that fly-covered, stinking stable next to our backyard. Standing there in his undershirt and rolled-up pants, Don Joaquin, the coachman, would wash his pair of horses down and comb their manes so lovingly they looked as if they were fresh from a first-class beauty parlor.

Don Joaquin would spend two or three hours a day on his daily chore of getting the carriage and horses ready. The horses kept whinnying and stamping their feet, when they were getting hitched up to the carriage. But my little first cousins had plenty of nerve and would help the coachman clean the mud off the wheels, grease the hood, clean the windows and lanterns, wash the manure and urine off that pair of animals, and put the harness on.

The old coachman, egotistical and with an inimical face, exploited the labor of these poor boys. He never thought of giving them a little ride, not even once around the block. Was he going to demean his coach by letting those dirty little ragamuffins in? He would throw them a peseta[1] from his perch on the coach box and then depart with a flourish of his whip, as if it were a magic wand that would bring him many colons that day.

His first trip each morning was to Dr. Esquivel's house, near Central Park. There the coachman was awaited by Doña Lupita and her pair of little blond girls looking like delicate angels. He came to give them a morning ride around Savanna Park.[2] That was why the coach had to be shining and impeccably clean—to be worthy of such distinguished clientele.

We children were by no means the only ones to admire the coaches of those days. My grandmother, my mother, and my aunts were all great admirers of those coaches and felt bitter envy and gnawing suspicion against the "society" people who always drove about in such handsome vehicles.

At that time, we were living on Tenth Avenue.[3] This was the street along which all the funeral processions of the rich folks and the middle-class people had to pass.

"Here comes a funeral! It's passing Our Lady of Sorrows Pharmacy right now!" shouted the children, announcing the grand show from the sidewalk.

Everybody in the family, big or small, rushed to grab the best place at the door or window so as to have a good view of the funeral carriages.

My aunts left their washtubs and hurriedly wiped the lather from their arms. My aunt Carmen stopped her sewing machine. My grandmother left the tortillas on the earthenware hearth, while my

---

[1] A peseta is equal to 25 centimos.

[2] The largest park in San José.

[3] A poor district on the southwest outskirts of San José

mother and my aunt Chana lifted the little ones up high. They were crying brokenheartedly because they could not see the very elegantly attired drivers setting the funeral pace for the two pairs of horses, who were drawing the hearse to wherever the illustrious deceased member of high society was going to his final resting place.

We were all pushing and shoving, crowding out onto the sidewalk, while my aunts dealt out their nips, pinches, and shoves. They, too, just like the children, wanted to enjoy the whole show down to the last detail.

Our eyes kept moving from side to side, looking at the elegant ladies decked out in gloves, veils, and black hats. They swayed mournfully in time to the slow rhythm of the trained horses. We stared at the sorrowing relatives bringing up the rear of the gloomy procession in their closed limousines. The gentlemen were all in black from head to toe. They wore eyeglasses with fine gold chains. Watch chains glittered across their respectable abdomens, imposing respect and silence. The coaches were completely covered with large wreaths bearing purple ribbons with the names of the institutions where the distinguished deceased had served. To us, the wreaths seemed like marvelous hanging gardens. They left a trail of fragrance in that barrio of so much misery and sin.

"Old fools! Let's go inside!" shouted my uncles as they reclaimed the lunches they had left behind. In the meantime, the hens and the tomcat had been up to their tricks and given the pots and pans forgotten on the hearth a good going-over.

All family activities ground to a halt when a high-class funeral cortege came by, for this always provided a really unique show that meant a break in the neighborhood's daily routine. Afterwards, it provoked the most picturesque comments, filled with rancor, mockery, and suspicion.

"What a world this is," Aunt Chana would say, "so tangled up and so uneven. Rich people have more money than they know what to do with. They go wrapped in cotton from the time they're born. They ride on wheels to the very mouth of the tomb. But when one of us poor people dies after suffering a whole life long, we just get kicked out of the way!"

"There you go again with your same old story. If it hurts your feelings so much, why the devil do you keep chasing out to see these f-----g funerals?" demanded my uncle Daniel, picking scraps of leather off his pants. "Quit whining and complaining," he added. "One thing is sure—we're all going to rot, the poor the same as the rich. So what's the big deal if they bury you in a marble tomb instead of out there in the plain dirt in the Calvo?[4]"

The same comments as always followed the chronicle of each funeral, the discussion taking on a certain philosophical aspect and invariably concluding with the words of the Bible: "It is easier for a camel to go through the eye of a needle, than for a rich man to enter into the kingdom of God."

*

At that time, riding in an open coach was one of the favorite pastimes during the popular celebrations at the year's end. The coachmen used to decorate their horses with garlands of colored paper and would hang tinkling bells around the horses' necks and ankles.

Coaches would parade along the main streets of La Puebla. They were full of people in festive mood shouting with Christmas cheer. We children were running about on the sidewalks enjoying a rare treat: the people in the carriages would throw confetti and streamers that were already sodden when we picked them up.

The price of a ride in one of the open coaches was five colons, an impossible luxury for the children of washerwomen and seamstresses. We knew very well indeed that the poor always have to be the eternal pedestrians everywhere in the world. "I've told you a thousand times," my mother would repeat, "money wasn't made for poor people."

This was a hard and cruel truth that we could not manage to grasp. It aroused envy and terrible feelings of rancor in our childish minds. These feelings were soothed a little whenever Aunt Chana

---

[4]The burial ground for the poor.

made her fantastic plans, dreaming that one fine day we would go with her for a ride in an open carriage and drive all over the city. Another day her dream would be that maybe we would win the lottery and could all go to Puntarenas to see the ocean.[5] Even grandma would go. At the age of sixty, she still did not know what that immense expanse of blue, warm, and salty water looked like.

What dreams that Aunt Chana had! Her fantasies lent wings to our imaginations and to our longings—the longings of children of poor families. We were always standing open-mouthed before so many lovely, marvelous, and exquisite things that are in the show windows of the civilized world, things that are forbidden and denied to millions of innocent children.

We were practical and realistic children. We had never heard of the story of *The Blue Bird*[6] nor of Cinderella's coach, conjured up from a pumpkin at the wave of a magic wand. And so we did not expect miracles or great strokes of fortune that could put porcelain dolls or colored balls into our hands, not to mention the grapes and rosy apples that made our mouths water when we passed by the show windows of the big department stores.

"That's not for poor kids like us—those things are for rich children, like Doña Lupita's fatty," I would explain to my younger brothers, sisters, and cousins. I spoke disdainfully, restraining myself with great dignity and with feelings of deep misgivings.

"Now, don't act silly. Shut up and hurry. We still have to go and deliver this big basket of tamales in Amón barrio," I reminded the youngsters, pulling them away from the polished glass of that show window on Central Street.

Aunt Chana's fantasies and stories lived on in the eyes and feet of my younger cousin Kiko, who could no longer contain his desire to ride in a coach—it had become an obsession with him. He would watch for the moment when he could get close to some coach and

---

[5]A bus trip of a few hours.

[6]*L'Oiseau bleu* (1909), a fairy play by Maurice Maeterlinck (1862-1949), a Belgian poet, dramatist, and essayist.

secretly sneak inside. On several such occasions, the coachman got rid of him with whip lashes, and Kiko came home with his knees all bloodied and scraped from the cobblestones of the street.

"What a pest this kid is! What a nuisance!" said my uncles, giving him a box on the ears and ordering him to carry out a flood of errands.

Like Kiko, we older children were also excited, caught up in the Christmas spirit, and enthusiastic about Aunt Chana's fantastic plans. Thinking about our unconquerable desire, we felt that it was harder to manage to get a coach ride than a trip to the moon. We did not resign ourselves or accept the unfair discrimination, when we could plainly see that even the prostitutes, who did no work at all, had the right to spend many hours riding in a coach. Finally we decided to take matters into our own hands and settle this urgent problem ourselves.

All the youngsters' troubles—our childish fears, worries, secrets, and distress, always so incomprehensible and alien to the grownups—were usually talked over while we were secluded in the outdoor toilet over the cesspool, which in those days was located at the far end of the backyards of the houses. That was where one afternoon my older cousin Julio and I plotted the strategy we would follow to make that impossible dream come true and to reach that far-off utopian goal. We had to make Aunt Chana's fantasies come true, even if by lying and stealing.

We finally decided to leap over all the obstacles and all the prohibitions and threats of my mother and my aunts. We boldly went to Fat Lips' house to tell her the problem and get two and a half colons from her to pay the cost of a coach ride for half an hour. Sentimental and generous, with the soul of a Good Samaritan, she understood our tragedy and, like a fairy godmother, she performed a miracle for us.

Among her clients, she had several coachmen friends who would willingly grant her every wish, so that we did not have to go into debt at all. Upon just a sign from her to one of her friends, we climbed into the open carriage, were grasped by her hands, and proudly made ourselves comfortable around her. Five of my little cousins, brothers, and sisters sat in the back seat. The others, displaying great courage, sat up in front alongside the coachman. For a half hour, our bliss was beyond words as, on that unforgettable late Christmas afternoon, we drove through the streets of the capital from Savanna Park to San Pedro of Montes de Oca.[7]

Of course, an adventure of this kind could not be kept secret. With the speed of lightning, concerned neighbors carried the tale to our house, where a battle like the one in San Quentin Prison was shaping up. The scandal could not have been more terrible, involving as it did the prestige of our entire family. The fact that five innocent children had gone for a coach ride with a prostitute was the ultimate depravity, the blackest besmirchment that had ever befallen our family. Puritanical and virtuous matrons forbade their children to play with us.

After tremendous reproaches and penalties, it was decreed in family council that for being the instigator of such an undertaking, poor Julio had to be put into the girdle of St. Francis. This was a white manila rope that had to be worn tied like a belt directly on the skin for a period of several months. As for me, my penance for having been the accomplice in such a diabolical and immoral plan was to go on my knees twenty times up and down the steps of Our Lady of Sorrows Church while reciting the prayer *"Mea Culpa."*

Aunt Chana had to accompany me to church for a number of days as eyewitness that my sentence had been carried out. But if the truth were told, she herself had been the real instigator, arousing and tantalizing us youngsters with her unrealizable hopes and dreams.

---

[7]About two miles from San José, San Pedro is the *cabecera*, or government seat, of Montes de Oca, a canton in San José Province.

6.   Give and Take

A gallery of pictures of the saints and images of the entire hierarchy representing the Heavenly Hosts presided over our home, nailed to our faded yellowish walls, from where they impassively viewed the trials and tribulations of our family life.

The pictures ranged from the Holy Trinity, very haughty, placed among the clouds, down to poor Lonely Spirit, serene in the flames of purgatory, performing miracles for those who suffer loneliness in this world.

There they were before our very eyes, the male and female saints world-famous for their miracles. All were praised by our neighbors and relatives, who testified on bended knees to the incomparable magic of every one of them in providing solutions to all the problems that Christians suffer from on this earth.

There was St. Caralampio, glorious priest and martyr, chief protector against the plague and all the dangers of contagion. It was to him that my aunts prayed when there was an epidemic of whooping cough or smallpox. A little further on there was Jesus of Good Hope. He was wearing one sandal, lavishly ornamented with pearls and diamonds, while the other foot was bare. This was because, one day, seeing the troubles of a devotee of his, he dispensed with the one sandal and allowed it to fall into this follower's hands. Next to this generous Jesus, who did not need those golden sandals for his cold and idle feet, rose the noble image of St. Joseph, standing on a cumulus cloud made up of thousands of letters. The faithful sent these to him from all the far corners of the earth, telling him their troubles and sorrows so that he might lay his hand on them.

My aunt Lola, the most ardent believer of us all, used to write at least a letter a month to the saint, although he never answered her.

But she unburdened her heart, telling him her secrets and inexpressible sorrows.

What did she care about Uncle Daniel's making fun of her as long as she was happy folding the thin paper and leaving it on the altar at St. Joseph's feet?

My grandmother, who was illiterate, used to say that answers from heaven did not come written on ordinary paper. They were divine replies sent from Our Lord by means of the blinking of the stars. You had to be ready and know how to read them on clear nights, those messages from heaven.

Next in the hierarchy came the Powerful Hand, with its five fingers emerging from among clouds, angels, and adorable cherubs, providing irrefutable evidence of its great power to stop the enemies and evil spells trying to get into our house. That was why we kept the Powerful Hand nailed firmly to the wall behind the street door, like a faithful watchman, in a special frame made of blessed palm leaf. We completed our defenses with this prayer to St. James of Gales:

"With the cross and the cypress, with the thirty-three angels in my company, with the cloak of Mary, let my body be protected. With the sword of St. Paul, let my body be defended from injustices and ill will. If my enemies have feet, let them not get to me; if they have a mouth, let them not speak to me; if they have eyes, let them not see me. With the handkerchief used to bind the eyes of Jesus Christ, I will bind the eyes of my enemies and the authorities that persecute me. Let the eyes of my enemies cloud over and let my eyes be washed with water of the Holy Spirit. The feet of my enemies will not be able to move, invoking the three nails with which Jesus Christ was crucified. May my enemies' arms become like long heavy branches, may their tongues fall asleep and their hands remain motionless. At the three signs of the cross, let my arms become light as straws, and let my enemies surrender at my feet."

St. Rita of Cascia, patron saint of desperate causes, was my mother's favorite, because she was the one who gave her strength to keep going, overcoming all the difficulties of this life, so hard and unjust.

All of us, some more, some less, had our preferences and sympathies for one saint or another.

I set my eyes on St. Hedwig, because she held in her hands a little gilded house with lovely balconies and windows and a little blue roof that ended in eaves that were a beauty. As she was the patron saint of homeless people, of those who lodge under the roofs of others, I said to myself, "I'll turn to her so she'll grant us a little house as beautiful as the one shining in her divine hands." I devoted myself with fervor to praying with deep faith in a novena to St. Hedwig. The miracle never happened, and we went on living in horrible houses, dark and sad. I felt cheated and was resentful toward the saint who would not hear my prayer. I tore the novena into a thousand pieces.

In our family, religion was a matter of give and take. Nobody engaged in philosophic deliberations of any kind. We lacked the time or the atmosphere for discussions of theology or the mysteries of the supernatural. As for novenas and the most basic religious rituals, we regarded them as possible recipes that could serve to solve the immediate problems and cares of our daily existence. We did not comply faithfully with Christian doctrine—months and months might pass by without our taking Communion or going to Mass.

When and where could we be meditating about problems of conscience? My aunt Carmen said it just right: "God, who sees all, knows very well that we live crushed under the yoke day and night. He'll have to pardon us our sins from up there."

The exhausting work barely left us time to say the Lord's Prayer at night, cross ourselves, and give thanks to God for "granting" us our daily bread. It was only when we felt ourselves overwhelmed that we occasionally resorted to novenas, which we generally gave up without finishing.

We often wished we could have talks with God and the saints so that we could complain to them about the injustices we were suffering in this world. That was why on some evenings when she was saying her prayers, my aunt Chana used to take the liberty of interjecting some words and sentences of her own, explaining to her favorite saints about the misfortunes and troubles that were befalling our home.

"St. Eligius, how much longer are you going to leave poor Andrés without a job? Virgin of Help, why don't you help Elías to quit his drinking?"

"And you, St. Antony, whatever are you doing that you're not sending poor Lola a good husband? She says that she has not gotten married because she never feels desire for a man, but you know that's nothing but a lie."

One hot afternoon in the month of March a more direct dialogue was kindled with the Most Holy Trinity. The atmosphere was being heated up by the coffee roaster and by the hearths filled with pots of tamales. The women were sweating beyond all endurance. A strong wind was just starting up when anguished screams were heard from my cousin Little Carlos, who had fallen from the top branch of the custard apple tree. My aunt Chana could not stand it anymore. Bathed in sweat and desperate, she ran out into the backyard with her fists raised high. And in a wrathful tone of protest, she scolded the Holy Trinity, whose Eternal Father was snoozing among the dark, threatening clouds which foretold lightning and thunder.

"What the devil are you doing, making yourselves comfortable up there in the clouds, instead of watching over these poor children here on earth while I'm earning our bread? What do you want? You want me to get caught in a draft and end up twisted and cockeyed forever?"

"Chana, don't speak blasphemy. That's no way to talk to the Holy Trinity! Don't you see that it's the Holy Spirit himself up there?" cried my aunt Lola, greatly frightened over my aunt Chana's lack of respect. Out of control and panting, as if she were in front of all the saints of the Heavenly Host, Aunt Chana summoned one and the other alike.

"It's not enough that we're poor. God sends us this cross of iron and does not even help us carry it. Instead, He loads even more on and then makes like He's deaf. So He's up there sitting on His throne of gold, and we down here, we're getting screwed in this hell of a life."

"Chana, shut up for the love of God. Have patience," urged my mother, grabbing her by the arm and giving her a glass of water with a few drops of essence of orange blossoms to help calm her rage. She was already showing signs of hysteria.

Two blinding flashes of lightning were followed by a heavy, thunderous downpour from the skies. The torrents of rain served to freshen that tense atmosphere, loaded with fears and forebodings of what might yet come down from on high as God's punishment for my aunt Chana's blasphemies.

Little Carlos kept on crying as he lay stretched out on a bench, while my grandmother put on compresses of camphorated alcohol. At the same time, she recited the Trisagion to calm down the tropical rainstorm, which, however, did not stop from three in the afternoon:

> "Holy! Holy!
> Lord God of Hosts,
> Heaven and earth are filled
> With the immense majesty of Thy glory...."

The frank and open challenge which my aunt had so disrespectfully flung at the Holy Trinity stirred me to the depths of my spirit. It let loose in my mind a storm of doubts and fears which ended in my agreeing completely with that courageous woman who had dared to openly give the Holy Trinity a good piece of her mind.

The saints were deaf, indifferent to our complaints. We recited novenas and more novenas, and not one problem was solved. We went on our knees ten times up and down the steps of Our Lady of Sorrows Church and in reply received neither a yes nor a no. When the Sweet Name of Jesus came around, we paid for a Hail Mary and dressed the children in purple tunics with yellow sashes,[1] and there was not the slightest change in our family fortune.

Distrust and suspicion created havoc in my soul. Then, since the same blood as Aunt Chana's also ran in my veins, I took the list

---

[1] In honor of the famous effigy of the Child Jesus wearing a purple tunic and yellow sash.

of saints and their specialties and crossed them out one by one, marking as void the long list of recommended saints who never cared to perform a single miracle for us, no matter with how much faith and ardor we prayed to them.

My uncle Daniel, who knew everything, used to say that to get the saints to perform miracles, you had to turn their pictures upside down and face them toward the wall.

7. I Don't Want My Daughter to be One More Beast of Burden

We poor are like the pebbles in the riverbed, we can't put roots down anywhere. We're condemned to wander along all the roads of the world, seeking some place where the sun shines down more kindly.

What didn't we have to do to earn our daily bread! No sentimentality can be permitted to attach us to a certain house, a certain barrio, certain friends, or certain memories. We can't be squeamish or lazy, we must always be ready to weigh anchor, be it midnight or high noon, rain or shine, whither and whatever the road.

Back in the year 1915, we had to go to live in the city of Heredia. In those days, it was very far from the capital, due to the lack of good roads and bus service. We had relatives there and good prospects for work, so that was where we moved.

One morning my father and I were leaving the market, loaded with sacks and baskets full of potatoes, corn, pork, and rolls of banana leaves.

It was Friday and we had to hurry to bring my aunts and my mother everything they needed to make the hundreds of tamales that had been ordered by various eating places and little groceries in the city.

Sweat was pouring off us as we picked our way down the rocky street to Hospital barrio under a burning sun that made the loads on our backs feel twice as heavy. Suddenly, I heard an affectionate voice saying,

"Good morning, my dear. Where have you been that I haven't seen you?"

Wiping the sweat from my forehead, I tried to locate the friendly voice that was calling to me from the distance, through all the confusion of the market. It was Miss Cristina, my teacher from fifth grade.

"Say hello to your teacher. Go on, answer her. Don't be bashful," urged my father, giving me a push in her direction.

"Good morning, Miss Cristina, how are you?" I timidly replied to her, meantime hiding my ugly, torn, and dirty shoes under the sacks and baskets.

"Well, now, sir, what are you intending to do with this little girl of yours? Are you going to leave her like this and not put her in the Normal School?[1]"

"It's very hard for us, Miss Cristina," answered my father, shifting a couple of enormous mesh cord bags on his shoulders. "The girl's the oldest and has to help us earn a living."

"God forbid!" said Miss Cristina. "You have to do everything possible so this girl can study. If you don't, sooner or later you'll regret that neglect."

"If it was up to me, I'd be very glad if she could study, so she wouldn't turn out as ignorant as we are. But you know, Miss Cristina, poor people like us can't afford such luxuries."

"No, no! No matter what, you must put her in the Institute. You know you can depend on me. I'll help you all I can. Take my advice—some day you'll thank me for it," added the good teacher as she took her leave from us, her soft hands caressing my dusty and sweaty braids.

"Thank you, Miss Cristina.... Adiós."

---

[1]The Normal School was the national teacher training institution of Costa Rica, operated by the Ministry of Education. The entrance requirement was graduation from six-year elementary school. Graduates of the institute's five-year course were appointed as teachers in the public elementary schools. The teacher training institutions have been incorporated into the state–supported universities, the Universidad de Costa Rica and the Universidad Nacional Autónoma.

We picked up our loads and quickened our pace.

"Did you hear what Miss Cristina said? Would you like to go to the Institute?" asked my father, surprised and excited.

"Oh no! I'd be ashamed," I answered. "And what about poor Mama? How can we leave her on her own with all that she has to do? And where would we get the money to pay for registration, for buying books, and all the rest of it?"

"What's this about being ashamed? Do you mean to say you're not as good as the other girls? Miss Cristina must have her good reasons for saying we shouldn't leave you without an education. Well, we'll see. One way or another we'll find a way out," said my father.

We went on walking, panting under the fiery rays of the summer sun. I followed along, stepping in the footprints my father's sandals were leaving in the burning hot dust.

"Well, well, girl. What are you thinking about? Why are you lagging so far behind? Don't you see how late it's getting?"

I made no reply. My mouth was dry, so dry, and for some reason the blood was buzzing in my head. The pebbles in the roadway all seemed to be turning somersaults and repeating Miss Cristina's advice: "You have to put this little girl in the Institute. Don't let her be wasted just like that."

Could it be that some day I would throw these sacks and these baskets to the devil and actually become a student at the Institute? Who was I to aspire to walk up that beautiful staircase that led to the door opening into those bright hallways, from where you could hear the lively shouts of the students? Could I too some day sit at one of those shiny desks and listen to the lectures held by the professors in front of hundreds of students? Could I go to the blackboard too, and could I sing those lovely songs with all the students—songs which my little brothers and sisters and I had listened to so many times from the street?

How dirty and ugly Papa's sandals were! How crooked and torn my poor black sandals were! What a long hard road to that broad, handsome stairway leading up to the Institute!

*

My mother was waiting for us impatiently, so she could get started on the big job of making the two hundred tamales on order. Fridays and Saturdays in our house meant speeded up work and increased noise and activity, Nobody had the right to lose even a minute. Everyone, big and small, had a lot to do. Since we all ate, we all had to redouble our efforts and, if necessary, work both day and night. It was the only way to make sure of our daily rice, beans, and sweet water.

The littlest ones got the jobs of washing the banana leaves and picking apart the strands, which had been left to soak in water overnight so they would be soft in the morning. We bigger children had mountains of potatoes and sweet peppers to peel, and we also delivered the orders to the grocery stores and eating places. The grownups carried out the jobs of cooking, washing, and grinding the dried kernels of corn, chopping the pork, fixing the rice, and putting the tamales together.

At that time, we had no electric grinders for corn, but my aunt Carmen's strong arms kept the wheel turning four to six hours at a stretch to crush the grains in the grinder. It was red and bore the trademark "Montezuma." The cornmeal dough came out white and hot, marbled with bits of spicy chili and fragments of ground, crisply fried pork rind.

"How delicious the cornmeal dough tastes in those tamales from the Gutiérrez family!" our customers would say.

My aunt Carmen's forehead, cheeks, and arms would be covered with sweat. When she took a break after such violent exercise, her muscles would continue to tremble like a vibrating motor. She would sit there briefly and chew a few grains of corn and a bit of candy while she caught her breath. Then she would go on again, earning her daily bread by the sweat of her brow.

There was no time to lose and no rest once my aunts and my mother came together like high priestesses, surrounded by jugs, pots, banana leaves, string, mountains of the cornmeal dough, pots of red rice, etc., etc., to undertake the big job of filling the hundreds of tamales in accord with all the rules of the culinary art. The tamales were soon going to be dropped one by one into the pots of boiling water that took up the whole hearth in my grandmother's kitchen.

My mother was the impresario who knew to perfection how to distribute the work among all the members of the family, assigning herself the chief responsibility and the hardest jobs. We all obeyed her orders, while she mixed huge amounts of the cornmeal dough, lard, and delicious spices in big buckets and washtubs.

The noise and crowds of the market had been left far behind. But in our house, it was no different or worse than in the city market.

My father and I dumped our whole load among some boxes in the kitchen, and the little ones ran to look for their beloved black taffy and other candy that we always brought them from the market on Fridays.

"We met Miss Cristina," began my father. He wiped the sweat off and looked for a bench where he could sit down to rest and tell what had happened, with full wealth of details.

"Miss Cristina says that we have to send this girl to the Teachers Institute, that it would be a terrible misfortune for us to keep her at home, what with her being so intelligent and studious. She promised to help us any way she could."

This recommendation from the good-hearted teacher fell like a bombshell in those surroundings, provoking the most vehement comments and protests. A great discussion broke out, and first one and then another analyzed the matter as if it were an affair of state. My shoemaker uncles, my seamstress aunts, my laundress cousin, my mother, and even my grandmother expressed their opinions. Everybody advised, discussed, shouted, ridiculed. They considered it completely out of place and alien to family tradition for any member of this working-class family to want to make a living in any way but by the labor of that person's own two hands.

"What's this nonsense about going around with books? That's just plain loafing," my aunt Chana declared, while she stirred the fire and made the sparks fly to lend emphasis to her words.

"Who's going to foist a little miss teacher on us here in this house? We don't have enough to buy beans with and we're going to waste money on such foolishness?"

"Haven't we always earned a living without needing any of those books, those plaques, or those diplomas?" shouted my uncle, hammering a moistened leather sole against the iron template.

"Those things are nothing but luxuries for the higher-ups. What that girl is going to turn into is a spoiled little señorita. She won't even know how to wash the plate she eats off of. Wait, you'll see," was the judgment my aunt Carmen expressed while she ground the corn.

"Haven't we been earning our living from the washtub and flatiron without having to bother with all those trifles?" added my oldest aunt, as she wiped the soapy froth off her dark-skinned arms with her apron.

Meanwhile, my mother lowered the pots of hot corn kernels, turned the pots upside down, and emptied them into huge, hard bamboo baskets, so she could wash the grains at the water trough. The water, turbid from the ashes, splashed over her feet in their big backless clogs.[2]

"Everything you're saying is one hundred percent correct. It's the pure and simple truth. Thanks to God and our labors, we haven't died of hunger and have been able to live honestly," said my mother, as she jerked the baskets back and forth under the water pipe. "But the truth is that everyone of us, from the oldest to the littlest, is nothing but a beast of burden. How many hours do we have to be glued to the washboard to earn a miserable fifteen pesos?[3] How many hours must we bend over the iron, the hearth, or the sewing machine just to make enough to buy rice and beans for the week? I know it sounds very conceited and ambitious of me, but I'm telling you there is no reason why our children should go on living in such a hell on earth. It's like an eternal curse hanging over us. I'm sick and tired of this dog's life of ours.

"Just tell me one thing: why wouldn't it be a lot better and make more sense to earn a hundred pesos working as a teacher than to make twenty pesos taking in ironing or sewing? Criticize and

---

[2]Ashes were added to the pots of water in which the dried corn kernels were cooked so that the skins on the kernels would be loosened and wash off in the rinsing.

[3]Slang term for "colons."

scream all you like, but I'm going to see to it that the girl is put into the Institute."

"Are you out of your mind? Where the devil are you going to get the money to pay for her registration, for books and supplies, and for all the nonsense and luxuries the Institute demands?" retorted my uncle, lighting himself a cigarette.

"Well, Daniel, if I have the strength to work and make a living, I'll have to find the strength to get the children out of this living hell too. Let me tell you that even if it means burning through my life thread, she's going to go to the Institute. This forehead that God gave me must be good for something, at least to keep me from leaving her to be one more beast of burden, like I've been. My girl is going to study, I don't care who screams and gets mad. I'm ready to sweat day and night over the scrubboard and flatiron for that."

Backed up by the hardness of those untiring arms, it was decided and decreed by my mother that I would go and study at the Institute and become a schoolteacher.

For the first time in this family, made up of shoemakers, washerwomen, seamstresses, and bricklayers, there was a break with the tradition of earning a living solely with one's own hands and labor.

This girl, a child of the common people, would earn a hundred colons or more working as a teacher. What good fortune! What a brilliant future for the child of this rebellious laundress, who had never been inside the building of the Teachers Institute. But she had grasped that going up that beautiful staircase would make it possible to go very far toward a new and better world, and one that her daughter had a right to!

Just what I would be learning in the classrooms of the Institute was not a subject for discussion. It had no significance. Nobody gave it a cumin seed's worth of thought.

Had anyone by any chance ever heard the word "culture" in that atmosphere, charged with greasy smoke, shouting, and anxiety? Could culture have found a place among so many black pots, among the washtubs, flatirons and baskets, sacks of coal, little children, mountains of firewood, and men and women working like slaves?

My mother's decision was carried out to the letter. There were her strong arms guaranteeing my studies at the Institute with her work from sunup to sunset. To the Teachers Institute, then, with the daughter of the washerwoman. On Monday, my father would go and register me.

*

Everyone was up earlier than ever before on that unforgettable Monday. Starting early in the morning, there was a coming and going in the whole house, as if it was a matter of preparing for some great event like a wedding or a journey abroad.

I began by scraping the mud from my poor shoes and, with the aid of water and shoe blacking, managed to get them to shine. "When I'm a teacher, I'll buy myself lots of shoes—white, black, and patent leather," I thought to myself, already dreaming of those hundred colons that I would some day hold in my hands.

"Come here so I can give those ears a good scrubbing and wash your hair," said my mother, unwrapping a bar of soap made of pork fat, the soap commonly used in all the homes of the poor.

Equipped with a large comb, water and the soap, she scrubbed my neck, my elbows, and my head with her hard hands of a good laundress who knew how to make the coarsest and dirtiest clothes in the world come out white as snow. Clean and well combed, with very tight braids, I was all ready to go from that humble little home to the Teachers Institute of Costa Rica.

My father put on his best shirt and cleaned his shoes, which he otherwise did only on Sundays, and I went to get my school certificate, which we kept safe in a box under the bed.

"Hurry now! Walk fast so you'll get there in good time," my mother ordered, trying to hide her feelings.

"So long, Mama...."

"So long, child, so long! May God go with you! Give my regards to Miss Cristina if you see her. Put the gate in place so the little ones can't get out in the street."

Out at the back of the yard on a water barrel lay the empty soap wrapper and the tin washbowl.

It was Monday. Ten dozen bundles of laundry were waiting at the washtub for my mother's strong hands. She had to keep on being a beast of burden all her life.

8. The Blue Pennant

My father, with a big basket full of cornmeal biscuits and cakes on his back, brought me to the Institute on the first day of school. Timidly and discreetly he came with me as far as the corner. I understood his gesture and thanked him in my heart that he did not go up to the door, for it made me feel bad that the students and teachers would see his humble appearance of a poor man and laborer.

That's how it is in this world. We poor people foolishly have to hide our poverty and be ashamed of it, as if it was a crime.

With cold hands and my face red with embarrassment, I ascended the twenty-four steps of the Institute's main staircase, a staircase that would lead me into a new, marvelous, faraway and strange world—the world of culture, science, and art, where idealism, spirituality, and so much more reigned that completely amazed me from the first day that classes began.

I was fourteen years old when I embarked on this great adventure, and the pores of my consciousness opened like a thirsty sponge. Everything seemed dazzling, new, strange, and completely alien to my life. It was as if I had entered a beautiful crystal palace, and I tried to walk on tiptoes. I timidly opened my eyes to see everything, but evaded the glances of the teachers, who were cordially greeting the students as we passed by in the corridors.

On the very first day, I went through all the halls, classrooms, laboratories, gardens, the library—everything. Finally I came to the *Sala Magna* [Great Hall]. *Magna*? What did that word mean? I did not know and did not dare to ask anyone. But as soon as I came to that huge hall, with its enormous white columns, large windows, and its whole atmosphere, I had the feeling I had entered a temple and could all but smell the odor of incense.

It was here in the *Sala Magna* that I heard for the first time the hymn of the Teachers Institute of Costa Rica. Alma Mater! Alma Mater! Another new word: Mater! Mater! What could that mean? The stanzas of the hymn sounded like church music to my ears. Without knowing why, when I heard the chorus being sung by hundreds of girls and boys like myself, a shiver went through my body from head to toe.

> "In sorrow or in triumph,
> The brilliance of thy star
> Will light our way,
> Our road will open."

"The brilliance of thy star will light our way, our road will open, our road will open...." Under the spell of those verses, I, innocent and devout, felt an indescribable emotion that penetrated every fiber of my soul and made my heart palpitate, as I entered for the first time into that new and beckoning world.

I came home happy that morning, carrying in my hands the little blue pennant of the Institute and the verses of that song full of hope.

My little brothers and sisters were waiting for me at the front door. Acrid, suffocating smoke and heat permeated the atmosphere, for the large bakery oven was furiously burning the logs needed to get the coals hot enough to bake the twenty large trays of biscuits, cornmeal cakes, and milk bread.

"How did it go?" asked my mother, while she wiped her hands on her heavy apron and looked me over from head to foot.

"It was marvelous, marvelous!" I replied, bursting with excitement and joy, already feeling myself to be a person of importance, different, distinct from this family of working people, who knew nothing about culture, for they lived in a different world.

I held the blue pennant up in front of the whole family and explained what it was all about. Then I read them the verses of the Institute's hymn, "Alma Mater," and emphasized the part about the brilliance of the star, for that had captivated me as much as if the song was about the Star of Bethlehem.

With remarkable respect, silence, and curiosity, they all listened to my account of what I had experienced on my first day of class at the Institute.

"And what are you going to do with that little flag? Where will you put it? Are you expecting to find any decent place for it here?" put in my uncle Daniel in a tone of disdain.

"Here's where I'm going to put it, nailed to this wall right near the window. Let everyone that passes by on the street see it. Then they'll know that here's where a girl lives that goes to the Institute."

"It's going to get all smoked up here," Daniel objected.

"That won't matter," I answered.

"Give a couple of nails here and bring a little hammer," my mother ordered Uncle Daniel, meantime sweeping the faded yellowish wall with a broom to make a place for the blue pennant.

My hands of a student united with my mother's to lovingly display the symbol, which from that day on would reign triumphantly in the midst of this humble home.

Oh, little blue pennant, you have accompanied me all my days and will accompany me into old age. I treasure you among the most precious souvenirs of my life, for in my youth, you were my banner of hope and unconquerable dreams.

9. From My House to the Institute, From the Institute to My House

From my house to the Institute, from the Institute to my house—every day I beat out a footpath of a thousand yards, bringing home an extraordinary profusion of experiences from school and returning to school involved with the numerous daily problems at home.

Although some foolish professor once said that you should leave your worries outside the classroom just as you would leave an umbrella or a hat at the door, I knew this was a lie. It was impossible to forget the landlord's blockade when he presented himself implacably at the end of every month to collect the rent. It was impossible to forget my little brother's illness when his screams pursued me one rainy day until I turned the corner of Flores Plaza.

To leave early each morning for the Institute with my books under my arm was a happy experience, a new joy each day, and an escape from that crushing, smoky house.

It was as if I were entering an unknown forest crowded with majestic oak trees, pines, and cedars. I took in deep breaths of oxygen from that atmosphere—so clean, bright, joyous, and vital—in the classrooms of the school. The atmosphere penetrated my whole spirit and opened the pores of my naïve and open soul to strange and fascinating directions.

How fortunate and how decisive for my life it was that I had teachers of the stature of García Monge,[1] Omar Dengo,[2] and Carmen Lyra,[3] whose great wisdom and generous hands shaped my destiny forever!

Oh, what an extraordinary and sublime miracle is the happy meeting between young souls, whose hearts are gifted, pure, and open, who know how to give themselves, with limitless passion, to cultural and exemplary civic efforts, as those teachers and writers of Costa Rica did.

Oh, unforgettable teachings, profound and simple, that sent shock waves of faith and enthusiasm through my soul of an adolescent girl! My spirit vibrated like a delicate green twig as I listened to the eloquent lectures of Omar Dengo and García Monge. Their clarion clear, courageous voices awakened in us young people the love of truth, culture, and justice.

With genuine devotion, I took and carried out to the letter the advice that my mother gave me every morning before I went off to school. I sharpened my pencil perfectly and copied into the white pages of my notebook those inspiring words that were little by little

---

[1]Joaquin García Monge (1881-1958), Costa Rican educator, writer, and journalist. Served as director of the Normal School and as Minister of Education. From 1919 until 1958, he published the *Repertorio Americano* (*American Repertory*), one of the most respected literary reviews in Latin America (Theodore S. Creedman, *Historical Dictionary of Costa Rica* [Metuchen, N.J.: The Scarecrow Press, 1977]).

[2]Costa Rican educator and essayist (1888-1928). A leader in educational reform efforts, he was director of the Normal School 1919-1928 (Creedman, 1977).

[3]Pen name of María Isabel Carvajal (1888-1949), educator, writer, and political leader. She has been described (Creedman, 1977) as "one of the most important women Costa Rica has produced." Active in educational issues, she started the first preschool in the country and helped found the National Library. She played a leading role in the struggle against the dictator Federico Tinoco, who resigned in 1919. An important leader in the Communist Party of Costa Rica, she was forced into exile after the 1948 civil war and died in Mexico City.

carving the facets of my spirit, molding my intelligence, my will, and the moral standards of a teacher and daughter of her people.

With mystical fervor, I guarded that notebook under my pillow and at night secretly read it again and again. I pored over the sayings that the professors of literature and history had quoted from the great thinkers, the classics, the heroes and liberators of Latin America, from the French Revolution, and from Abraham Lincoln.

Just as stars first appear timidly here and there in the sky in the haze of twilight, so there began to appear in my gray skies those beautiful faces with broad foreheads and vigorous heads. I imagined them to be set in resplendent gold and silver, like the wonder-working saints that my aunt Chana worshipped and adored in her gallery of inexpensive engravings and color prints that she bought in the city markets.

The incandescent, tender, and impassioned thoughts of José Martí[4] captured my soul forever. My soul in its hard shell, buried in clods of earth, blossomed into hope and faith at the vision conjured up by his immortal poetry:

> "With the poor of this earth
> I want to share my fate.[5]"

"With the poor of the world," I said to myself, "that means with us, with us living in this filthy barrio, in these ugly, crumbling houses; with those who work like beasts of burden from sunrise to sunset; with all the poor people of this world, with all of us—big and small, black and white. It means taking action on the side of all of us poor."

---

[4]Cuban poet, writer and revolutionary (1853-1895), who died in battle in Cuba, fighting to free Cuba from Spain.

[5]One of José Martí's many books is *Versos Sencillos* (*Plain Poems*), consisting of 45 poems of from two to seven stanzas each. It was published in 1891 in New York, where he lived 14 years in exile. After his death, three of these stanzas, set to a Cuban street song, became "*Guantanamera*," popularized by Pete Seeger and the Weavers over half a century later.

Oh, simple and immortal words that have awakened the consciousness of millions and millions in the world and that, like a ray of light, pierced me to the depths of my soul. Martí's words gave me an understanding of my own self and where I belong in our unjust and inhumane society!

Poor though I was, those words of the great Cuban poet sank deep roots into my soul. From that time on, I have vowed over and over again to devote my life to the people of my class, to stand with the common people.

Don Joaquin García Monge, understanding very well that a spark of the poet's thought had caught fire in my soul, made me a present of a beautiful portrait of Martí, with another inspiring verse, which served to confirm the budding convictions of my independent-minded and rebellious spirit:

> "I know of a deep sorrow
>   And of suffering beyond words.
>   The enslavement of mankind
>   Is the world's great sorrow."

Every word of these lines lacerated my soul, wounding it to the quick, and added to my romantic passion for justice and liberty.

Don Omar Dengo put into my hands *La Edad de Oro*, by Martí.[6] His historical tales about Father las Casas,[7] Bolívar,[8] and the

---

[6]Founded in July, 1889 in New York City, *The Age of Gold* was a monthly illustrated children's magazine. Martí wrote and edited the magazine, which had stories and poetry about art, music, history, science, fairy tales, and much more. Financial backing was withdrawn after four issues. These four issues make up the book.

[7]Bartolomé de las Casas (1474-1566), Spanish Dominican missionary and historian. Worked to improve the conditions of Indians in the Spanish colonies in Latin America.

[8]Simón Bolívar (1783-1830), Venezuelan general and revolutionary, who led the South American colonies in revolt against Spanish rule.

curate Hidalgo[9] inflamed my impassioned girl's heart almost to frenzy and kindled my enthusiastic support for the struggles that have made it possible for people all over the world to win independence and liberation.

I put Martí's portrait and immortal verse on the wall over the head of my bed.

"What kind of crazy idea is this?" asked my uncle Daniel, surprised and finding it strange.

"That's José Martí, the liberator of Cuba, a writer and famous poet," I answered, in that certain tone of voice of a learned person showing off being educated and able to give lectures to those ignorant shoemakers and seamstresses who did not know—in those days—where the island of Cuba was and who much less could know anything about the poets, writers, or liberators of Latin America. How could they, when not one person in the family had gone through grade school and when there had not been a single book in the house on history or literature?

Everyone in the family was curious and interested to know who that gentleman with the beautiful, serene forehead could be. They stood together in front of Martí's portrait and listened with respectful attention to my learned explanations.

I promised the children to read them two of Martí's stories in verse that evening: *"Los Zapaticos de Rosa"* ["The Little Pink Slippers"][10] and *"Los Dos Príncipes"* ["The Two Princes"].[11] My aunt Chana and my uncle Daniel came and listened with respect and admiration.

---

[9]Hidalgo y Castilla (1753-1811), Mexican priest, patriot, and revolutionary.

[10]A poem in which a child gives her new shoes away to another girl whose feet are bare and cold.

[11]A short poem inspired by the U.S. writer Helen Hunt Jackson. Martí admired her because she championed the cause of Native Americans. He translated her novel *Ramona* into Spanish.

10. "In Angello cum Libello"

In a corner with a book

— à Kempis[1]

Like plows turning up deep furrows in the black fertile earth, ready for abundant germination, thoughts entered my head in throngs, whirling around in my mind of a girl of seventeen. There were new ideas, strange ones, tormenting thoughts, thoughts causing me anguish, and romantic, bold and passionate thoughts.

Diminutive books in elegant editions of the great authors from around the world, classic and modern, would fall into my hands whenever some professor or schoolmate would lend them to me. My most ardent wish was for money to buy at least *Platero y Yo* [*Platero and I*], by Juan Ramón Jiménez.[2] We had read the book in Spanish class, and I was filled with tenderness and love for the immortal little burro.

How could I explain to my mother, sweating and overburdened with exhausting work, my desire for this book and for so many

---

[1]Thomas à Kempis (1379?-1471), German ecclesiastic and author. From an inscription, attributed to him, on his picture at Zwoll, Holland: "Everywhere have I sought rest and found it not, except sitting apart in a nook with a little book."

[2]Mexican author (1850-1910), one of Latin America's most popular writers.

others that I wished I could have? A few weeks earlier, my father had made a great to-do about buying me a secondhand *Larousse* dictionary, which fell into our family surroundings like some intruder.

Without understanding its importance or the need I felt for that little book, my mother agreed and gave me the money to satisfy my craving. I ran and bought a modest edition of *Platero y Yo*. Just about then, we had happened to land a good contract to supply cornmeal biscuits and sweet corn cakes, so everyone was in a good mood. We could have some centavos to squander on a book nobody knew anything about or what use it had.

It was with that old dictionary, with *Platero y Yo*, and with *La Edad de Oro*, by Martí, that I started my first library. I kept it in a little box of white pine that I nailed to the wall between the window frame and the front door.

I enlarged my arsenal with the *Repertorio Americano* and the beautiful editions of the *Colección Ariel* [*Ariel Collection*] and *El Convivio* [*The Companion*], published by Professor García Monge, the unforgettable and patient sower of ideas. With naïve simplicity, I cared for and guarded my library like a treasure, just as my aunt Chana did with her enormous collection of prayers and novenas.

In angello cum libello. This motto appeared in Latin in tiny letters on the books distributed everywhere with tireless energy by Professor García Monge. I repeated it a thousand and one times, just as it stood in Latin, while I imagined a little corner—pleasant, secluded, fresh, and clean—where I could sit down for some peace and quiet. There I would find a sheltering silence and for long hours could read so many beautiful stories, so many lovely poems, tales, and fables that would set me to marveling and would take hours of leisure time. Even a small space of a square meter would do, without flies and smoke. There I could curl up awhile with a book in my hands, just as the mystical German's motto suggested.

I was a penniless student, idealistic and utopian, who wanted to turn that motto of à Kempis into reality in my house. But my home was so different and so far removed from the peaceful stillness and unworldly atmosphere of convents, filled with light and shadow and inviting to serene and quiet meditation.

"You poor simple girl!" the big oven seemed to be shouting at me, with its huge gullet wide open, smoky, thirsty, and carpeted with red-hot coals. It was waiting to swallow the portions of white dough for the cornmeal biscuits and sweet corn cakes, which were quickly baked by that oven, the lord and master of the enterprise that dominated our family economy.

Hard reality won out. It was impossible to have the right to a quiet corner where I could sit and read for hours at a time, as à Kempis proposed.

I felt an irresistible urge and a duty to share my new feelings and new knowledge with the poverty-stricken people of my home, enslaved by exhausting labor, in which they fulfilled to the letter the biblical injunction "Thou shalt earn thy bread by the sweat of thy brow."

It was thanks to the sweat of those brows and those tireless arms that I was giving myself the luxury of being able to study at the Institute, of being able to sit down for long hours, listening to lectures on literature, history, science, and psychology. Many times my conscience shuddered when scruples seized me at the thought of the commotion and rush of work going on at home, while I sat listening to stories, history, and the mythology of Greece and Egypt, which extolled the heroism and deeds of great figures of antiquity.

One day I even interrupted my professor of literature, Carmen Lyra, to confront her poetic accounts of the heroes of mythology with my own account of the exemplary and heroic lives of my mother and my aunts. Such was the ever present contradiction being debated in my mind as I was being propelled from a proletarian atmosphere to a new world that was different and distinct, where my mind was being influenced by culture and study.

Filled with remorse and scruples, I decided to set up my own chair of education there at home with my own plain working people. I was gaining ascendancy as the only person in the family with an education. I could correctly explain many things which came up for discussion in the family circle around the shoemakers' benches or near the oven, where its flames threw silhouettes of the children, my mother, and my grandmother onto the kitchen wall, like Chinese shadow play.

My authority kept growing with this audience of people who were uneducated but intelligent and curious, as I explained the theories of Galileo and Copernicus about the solar system, or when I expounded on the theories of the phenomena of lightning, of the tides, or the phases of the moon.

Of course, I was careful to be discreet with this public of mine, never explaining to them Darwin's theory of the evolution of the species. I knew that from the pulpits of Heredia many dangerous excommunications and damnations had been pronounced against those who tried to spread such theories. Besides, I was distrustful myself and a little afraid of the explanations given by some of the materialistic professors, who sowed doubts and reservations in the minds of the young students.

As a fourth year student, the scope of my knowledge impressed itself to overflowing on the minds of the whole family when, openmouthed, they heard me say a few elementary phrases in French or English. The children learned to say "Good morning" and *"Bonjour,"* and every morning we greeted each other indiscriminately in either of the two languages.

There was a good deal of admiration mixed with fondness for novelty, envy, and at times an unspoken fear that I would become conceited and betray the traditions of our family, which had always been made up of people who were sweaty and robust, with strong, callused hands, and who were proud of their heritage from the common people.

My mother soon put the brakes on any such risk from me. With great wisdom, and moved by necessity as well, from the first day of vacation she handed me a huge work quota in the bakery, which I fulfilled punctually, working eight and ten hours a day.

Meanwhile, in my mind I was reworking and reviewing what I had learned in the past lecture year. I thought over the most important lesson of all: to know how to go from the gleaming, varnished desk of the academy to the humble wooden bench and to earn my daily bread by the sweat of my brow the same as my mother, my aunts, my father, and all the generations that have gone before me.

Our cottage industry grew daily. Those were the years of the First World War. No more wheat flour came from the United States, and for that reason corn was the raw material that made up for the lack of wheat bread. Business was splendid for our bakery. We had the best customers in Heredia because our cornmeal bakery goods and ring biscuits were made by my mother from recipes she had invented herself. Her corn rings were unique in their flavor and degree of toasted crispness. When the ring was broken for dunking, it came apart and swelled up into savory bits that filled the cup of hot black coffee.

The "society" people gave us large orders for biscuits, which they took along to their estates for the summer. My younger brothers delivered the biscuits in coarse cotton sacks to the leading families of the city, all of them cash customers.

We took no breaks. Many times even during Holy Week, for instance, we were working all night long to fill the orders and contracts that my father brought in from all over the city.

The success of our enterprise was reflected in my library: my books could no longer fit into the little white pine box. Because I worked very hard in the bakery, my mother rewarded me by giving me money to buy the books I needed.

Just as the big logs of black wood and golden *guachipelín* came in through the door to heat that oven, four square meters in area, so through the same door to my library came the most varied and great authors of world literature, recommended by professors at the Institute and by student friends: Tolstoy, Emerson, Carlyle, Tagore, Ruskin, Dickens, Darío,[3] Wilde, Mistral, Rodó,[4] Fray Luis de Leon,[5] and many others. They found their place in new boxes that protected them from the dust and smoke that we breathed in the air of that factory for cornmeal biscuits and sweet corn cakes.

---

[3]Nicaragua's most celebrated poet, Rubén Darío (1867-1916) was founder of the modern school of poetry in Latin America.

[4]José Enrique Rodó (1871-1917), Uruguayan essayist.

[5]Spanish poet, translator of the Bible, and didactic writer (1527?-1591).

The burning logs crackled in the oven, always voracious, the flames causing the sap in the freshly cut wood to sizzle in boiling hot tears. Just so, my tender and pure soul crackled, amazed and lost in the writings of those authors who opened deep crevices in my virginal thoughts. Fortunately, I was free from philosophic prejudices and the burdens of false erudition.

Among such authors was the caustic Almafuerte,[6] with his *Imprecaciones y Lamentaciones* [*Curses and Lamentations*], incandescent and harsh, rubbing salt into my independent and rebellious soul:

"In order to rise to Jesus it is necessary to descend to Dimas,[7] and to get to Dimas one must leave the unbreathable ether of the innocent and pure far above.

"Do not believe the sermon of that abbot perfumed with heliotrope, who climbs up into his pulpit with his heart still full of suave impressions from the Conferences of St. Vincent de Paul and the charity balls of the duchesses, and who then passes like a Caesar, sweating in his lacings before that most elegant multitude, whose artistic feeling he has produced and whose admiration he has won.

"Believe, yes, in the real St. Vincent de Paul, yes, in the apostleship of that blind priest of charity, rendered insane by evangelisation, who first launches forth into the deserts of Africa and then plunges into vice in the lowest dives in the city, which are the deserts of civilization, and finally leaves, tortured by doubts, covered with curses, and consumed with remorse."

Almafuerte, *"El Misionero"* ["The Missionary"]

---

[6]Pseudonym of Pedro Bonifacio Palacios (1854-1917), Argentinean poet.

[7]According to Christian belief, Dimas was the thief who was crucified at the same time as Jesus and taken to Heaven by Jesus.

There too was Darío, with his *Motivos del Lobo* [*Motives of the Wolf*], throwing shadows of pessimism and desolation over my mind. On the other hand, there were "The Happy Prince" and "The Birthday of the Infanta," marvelous stories by Oscar Wilde. I read them to my young brothers, sisters and cousins with incredible dramatics, even making them cry as they lay huddled together on the hard, dilapidated bed.

Further on, there was *The Crescent Moon* and *The Gardener*, by Tagore, whose poetic mysticism was celestial music that fell like fresh dew on my soul, so alien to the spiritual philosophy of the great Hindu poet.

Like nuggets of gold among the pebbles and sand of the river, *Leaves of Grass*, by Walt Whitman, came into my hands. There are providential people and books that cross our path and that, like precise compasses, determine our destiny forever. They blow away the fog and empty talk that surrounds us and clarify our thinking, giving our consciousness a sure and definitive direction. This occurs at around the age of twenty years when we are wandering about, lost among the shadows and clearings of so many philosophies that dazzle and daze our minds.

Leaves of Grass, with its powerful "Song of Myself," shook me to the very depths of my being, to the delicate roots of my incipient philosophic thinking. A vital, fresh, vigorous and clear sap circulated through my veins, washing away the doubts and fears, pessimism and prejudices, which were weakening and undermining my spirit.

I was wandering about off the track, trying to nestle my soul in the clouds "far from the madding crowd" among fantasies and distant utopias. Now I came rolling, jumping and leaping, to fix my feet firmly on this earth, on which I had to live out my life like all mortals, at the side of all the people, good and bad, and without squeamishness or reservations.

My soul was forever freed from impediments upon the incantation of Whitman's immortal verses, which from then on became my new gospel, followed with passion and boundless devotion.

I bought a small, fine notebook with gold edging, and in perfect lettering I copied down the thoughts of his that impressed me most:

"I have said that the soul is not more than the body,
And I have said that the body is not more than the soul,
And nothing, not God, is greater to one than one's self is,
And whoever walks a furlong without sympathy walks to his
    own funeral drest in his shroud,...."

"Why should I pray? why should I venerate and be
ceremonious?"

"I exist as I am, that is enough,
If no other in the world be aware I sit content,
And if each and all be aware I sit content."

"I believe in the flesh and the appetites,
Seeing, hearing, feeling, are miracles, and each part and tag
    of me is a miracle."

11.   Shame

Thou shalt love beauty, for it is the shadow
of God over the Universe.[1]

— Gabriela Mistral

One evening, as I was leaving the Institute library together with
some girlfriends from school, Don Omar came over to our group to
talk a few minutes with us. As it was getting dark, he politely offered
to accompany those of us who lived further away, toward Heredia
Hospital barrio.

Without thinking of the kind intentions of this teacher friend, a
true educator of the youth, I felt my heart flip over and was seized
with fright and indescribable embarrassment and shame, for I
realized that Don Omar would be walking with us along the very
same muddy paths over which I went every day from my house to the
Institute.

On that evening, I wished that the earth would swallow me up,
that something unheard of and terrible would happen—an earthquake, a fire—something, my God, that could keep the professor
from reaching the rickety door of my dirty, dark house, which was
like so many others on the south side of the city.

---

[1]From *"Decálogo del Artista"* ("Ten Commandments of the Artist").

Don Omar did not notice how upset I was and continued walking and talking with us. In the group, there were three girls who lived across from my house. By great good luck, my door was shut.

On hearing the noise of our talking, my mother and my aunt Chana looked through a crack and saw the neighbor students from our barrio.

Abruptly, I said good-by to Don Omar, opened the door with a push and got inside, panting, with my soul hanging by a thread.

"What time d'you call this to be coming home? Where'd you come from? Who was that man talking to you? Don't you realize it's almost nine o'clock at night? What will people say? That I'm an old madam!" shouted my mother in a fury.

"It's Don Omar, Mama, the director of the Institute. You should hear how beautifully he speaks—you could spend hours listening to him talk."

"What the devil has he got so much to talk about?" inquired my aunt, intrigued and suspicious. "If he had to get up early like me, he wouldn't give his tongue free rein till midnight."

"And what do you want them to talk about? Books and more books? Do you see how that girl keeps our house? Even under the bed she keeps those confounded papers that are coming out of my ears already," said my mother, annoyed because I had come home so late and, as if that was not enough, accompanied by a man who was a complete stranger to her.

"Lucky for us that gentleman came at night and couldn't tell what a pigsty we live in," added my aunt, while she beat the dust out of the mattress.

"Don't you come home again at this time of night, and certainly not with strange men," said my mother in a severe and dogmatic tone of voice.

"Now you see? I told you so! She was so shy and such a good girl! And now she is getting ruined, loitering about on the streets like all those girls at the Institute. Wouldn't it be better if she stayed home with us and worked here without running any risk?" said my aunt, greatly worried.

Bewildered and confused by my mother's unjust reprimand and at the same time recalling the interesting talk we had had with Don

Omar along the way, I stayed awake a long time without being able to understand my mother's and my aunt Chana's prejudices.

For over a week I passed through the corridors and classrooms of the Institute, trying not to show my face to Professor Dengo. With his own eyes and discreet heart, he had discovered where his pupil lived, a girl with a frown who unblinkingly listened to his marvelous lectures and speeches, which were accompanied by gestures that enchanted her and sent her soul soaring like a kite, far, very far, above the roofs of the city.

The following Monday, Don Omar gave a truly beautiful talk in which he introduced us to *"Decálogo del Artista"* ["Ten Commandments of the Artist"], by Gabriela Mistral. It was like a kaleidoscope in which the colors kept changing before my eyes, awakening my imagination and fantasy.

When I got home, I tried to remember her beautiful and profound ten commandments, which were beyond the comprehension of a poor student who was barely beginning to glance timidly into the byways of art.

I learned Gabriela Mistral's ten commandments by heart, just as I had learned the Ten Commandments of God's Law without understanding them. I compared her ten commandments with the laws of Moses and took hers as a new declaration of faith, which filled my ears with enchantment:

> "Thou shalt love beauty, for it is the shadow of God over the Universe."

But the shadow of God was restricted, short, and far away. It did not reach as far as the slum barrios of the south side of the city. Again, I saw everything around me: my smoky house, the narrow, dirty street, sweating workers rushing from place to place, the dirty faces of the children playing on the sidewalks, the mangy dogs looking for a bone to chew, while I was making superhuman efforts to understand the philosophy of that beautiful and profound prose.

It was many, very many, years later before I at last understood that the spiritual enjoyment of art and culture, of progress and civilization is rationed or completely denied to millions and millions of people in the world.

12. Vocation

Lord! You that have taught, forgive me for teaching, for bearing the title of teacher, that you bore on earth.

Grant me the unique love of my school, that even the burning of beauty shall not be able to rob me of tenderness at all times.

Show me in my time what is possible in your Gospel, so that I never give up fighting for it every day and every hour.

— Gabriela Mistral[1]

As big sister to seven brothers and sisters and as the oldest of eleven cousins, from a very early age on I had been leader of this throng of children, the abundant harvest of the unquestionable and proven fertility of my mother and my aunts. They were vigorous women with wide hips and full bosoms, who brought children into the world every year without thought or talk about biological theories, morals or economics.

The babies came as they would. It was another one of the many duties and obligations that the women of the family fulfilled without complaint, without protest, always finding a little spot for the newest

---

[1]From *"La Oración de la Maestra"* *("*The Teacher's Prayer*").*

offshoot of this fertile, inexhaustible stock which spread like the purslane plant.

Perhaps it was the training provided by playing nursemaid to a flood of youngsters of all ages, as well as the responsibility that fell on my shoulders since I was seven years old, that in part decided my future vocation of teacher, and I took it to heart as earnestly as a novice about to put on the nun's habit.

It was like honey on pancakes when one day *"La Oración de la Maestra"* ["The Teacher's Prayer"], by Gabriela Mistral, fell into my hands. I immediately learned it by heart. It imbued me with such fervor that I decided to go to the Heredia Parish Church and recite it, which I did with deep devotion. Still a young adolescent, I implored the Lord to help me carry out the apostleship that I was taking into my hands.

One evening I recited Mistral's poem to my mother and aunts. They listened to it as they would to any new prayer, but without comprehending the philosophical meaning of that inspired prose.

"And is this a prayer that has been blessed? Is it all right to recite it like other prayers?" my aunt Carmen asked me, holding back the sewing machine wheel and speaking mistrustfully.

"Yes, of course," I assured her, in a gesture of inexplicable audacity that left no room for the slightest doubt.

Armed with this prayer which had penetrated so deeply into my thinking, I felt myself bold, courageous and chosen by God to carry out the apostleship of teaching and to guide broods of children of my native land into the world of knowledge and culture. I felt myself empowered and capable of carrying all the children in the world on my back, just like the giant St. Christopher did when he carried the child Jesus on his shoulders.[2]

---

[2]Legend has it that St. Christopher was carrying a child across a ford and, despite his gigantic stature and great strength, nearly fell under the child's weight. The child was Christ, carrying the weight of the whole world in His hand.

13.   The Hole in the Doughnut

The lovely children's rounds by Gabriela Mistral, the beautiful prose of *The Crescent Moon*, by Tagore, the story of the school of Santiniketan and of Yasnaya Polyana,[1] and the theories of Rousseau, Pestalozzi, and Froebel created a thousand fantasies in my mind. These made me dream of utopian projects to which I would devote my whole life, just as those great educators of humanity did.

The pedagogical sciences, children's literature, psychology, the history of education—these were studies that I found completely absorbing. They opened up vistas of the marvelous and creative capacity in the world of children and their wonderful possibilities as the reserve and future of a perfect, just, free and happy humankind. It would be like an Arcadia, which the teachers would be able to create, turning into reality the theories that we had learned in those unforgettable classes at the Institute.

---

[1] In 1901, Rabindranath Tagore (1861-1941) opened a small experimental school at Santiniketan ("Abode of Peace"), a family-owned tract near Bolpur, north of Calcutta.

In 1859, Leo Tolstoy (1828-1910) started a school for peasant children at his family estate of Yasnaya Polyana ("Ash Glade"), near Moscow. In 1862, he set up more schools in neighboring villages and founded a periodical, *Yasnaya Polyana*, to reach a wider audience about his ideas on education.

Both Tagore and Tolstoy anticipated a number of modern educational practices.

Absorbed in reading the books on education, I made fantastic plans, dreaming of a little rural school "far from the madding crowd," set in a woods filled with birds and flowers, where I, like a simple shepherdess, would care for these hypothetical children as if they were cherubs just descended from heaven. With deep affection, I would try out on them the most modern pedagogical theories in vogue at the time.

But dreams remain dreams. In contrast to the books and the professors' expositions, I had to consider my own reality, my own life as a girl and a child of the common people. In the daily lives of my mother, my aunts, and our neighbors in the barrio, their sole pedagogy in bringing up their children consisted of screaming, beatings, a box on the ears, pinches, scoldings, and threats about the devil and hell.

The deep clefts between theory and reality shattered in my mind the logic that seemed so clear and simple in the professors' lessons, lessons that I listened to with a certain suspicion, pessimism, and distrust, as if I were at the foot of an enormous slope which was impossible to climb. From my lowly position, I considered all the problems in the blackest terms. I could see no horizons, perspectives, or solutions. This tenacious obstinacy earned me the reputation of seeing only "the hole in the doughnut," according to what my dear professor Don Omar used to say.

I felt an unappeasable, urgent desire to put into practice all those interesting pedagogical theories, beginning with the children in our own family. Those sweaty, mischievous youngsters escaped from me like rabbits, running off to play in the barrio or the nearest open pasture.

I had to make the test and prove my authority as a teacher and a learned person, who was bringing home the most modern and revolutionary pedagogical methods. I had to win these youngsters over, applying all the scientific techniques that I had learned from the books on child psychology.

I cleared out part of the space where we kept our firewood, at the back of the open storage shed. There, using benches and boxes and an old board for a blackboard, I set up my first classroom and gave my first classes in accord with the arts of modern pedagogy.

"What witchcraft could that girl be using to keep those pesky kids so quiet?" asked my mother, secretly looking in to see, while I was reading them the first pages of the book *Heart*, by Amicis.[2]

"Those darn kids! I thought there must be some kind of magic going on," added my mother, surprised to see the effects of my teaching. It was magic derived from studying the methods that I wanted to try out on the minds of these youngsters, enslaved by the austerity of poverty and work. They were free from sentimentality and reflection, but perhaps filled with anxiety, envy, repression, and suspicion.

*

On arriving home from the Institute one afternoon, I found my ten-year-old cousin Kiko on his knees in the shed. His father had ordered this punishment for the duration of three hours because Kiko had lost two colons on his way home from the market.

Here he had to remain alone, isolated from everyone, in the dark, after having gotten a whipping that left large purple marks on his legs and thin buttocks. Tears were running down his face as he begged forgiveness for his crime. The punishment had to be carried out. No one dared to change it because of the implacable authority of Ramón, my uncle by marriage. He was a bricklayer, as rough and hard as a rock and like the cement his tough hands handled. No one spoke. The children were as silent as at Mass. From a distance, they watched poor Kiko being subjected to torture. The women were biting their lips in anguish at the sight of the poor innocent creature suffering such punishment.

The boy's tears fell on my heart like a bolt of lightning, kindling my anger. With great pedagogic authority, I took Kiko by the arm, raised him, and hid him behind me to protect him from his father's savage temper.

---

[2] Edmondo de Amicis (1846-1908), Italian author. In his 1886 book *Cuore* (*Heart*), Amicis suggests how an educational system might be developed to create a socialist community.

"In the name of all the devils! Who's boss in this house, this skinny girl or me?" my uncle Ramón shouted, giving me a shove so he could grab the boy, who was clinging to my blue skirt like a monkey.

"You're not boss over anything here! Go to the devil a thousand times! You act like a big bully with poor Kiko because he's only a weak little child!" I replied. I was furious and defended the sniveling youngster with unheard-of boldness. The boy was trembling and screaming exaggeratedly, finally causing the dramatic intervention of the whole family.

First one, then another joined in the dispute, taking sides for or against that insolent, bold girl who was dragging the authority of this stern bricklayer through the mud. He was a family head who used the strap left and right, as if he were an animal trainer, using the only method he knew of to impose his authority.

The most absurd opposite opinions on the education of children and on the authority of the parents and the respect due to older people from children were discussed that afternoon, in view of the very grave incident which I had provoked when I interfered with the sentence pronounced on poor Kiko. Now amazed and safe behind me, Kiko was wiping his dripping nose and tears on my discolored skirt.

In the end, my standpoint won out because it was reasonable and fair, so I could count on support from my mother and Aunt Chana, whose judgments always carried the most weight in the bosom of the family.

My grandmother called Kiko aside to the kitchen. There at the hearth she gave him a little snack made of a toasted tortilla and fried cheese, trying to help him forget his troubles. In front of the expectant and envious eyes of the other youngsters, he gulped it down in one swallow and went out to play tag, happy and triumphant.

I went back to my books that evening when everything had quieted down in the house. Next day I was going to take an examination in child psychology and another one in methodology. The battle I had won that afternoon to protect poor Kiko seemed to be reflected in the pages of my textbooks, lending me an extraordinary feeling of clarity and clairvoyance. I felt confirmed in my stand as a loyal and faithful student facing my first struggles in defense of the principles of my incipient teaching philosophy.

When I got up next morning, my mother, greatly worried, told me that Ramón and my aunt Carmen, his wife, had decided to leave. They considered my intervention in defense of Kiko as an insult beyond measure and a great humiliation to them. Ramón could not continue to stand for my insolence or my pretentiousness. He found a job in the port city of Limón and they moved there.

This new situation caused an acute crisis in our family economy. We alone could not keep up the rent for the house. Even though the house was not nice, on the other hand it did offer in exchange the convenience of having the bakery facilities there. We were forced to leave Heredia and look in new directions. Luckily, a friend of my father offered him a good contract to provide meals for the prisoners at the penitentiary and to do the laundry for the soldiers at the artillery barracks. These magnificent prospects opened the road for us to again return to the capital. That was in 1922, the year of my graduation.

14.   Graduation: 1922

And so we came back again to San José, once more to La Puebla barrio. It was more civilized now, for the red-light district had been relocated to other barrios of the south side of the capital. In view of this change, Porfirio Brenes School had been built in the neighborhood of Our Lady of Sorrows Church.

Once again we had the lord and master of the house as lodger with us—the big oven for baking cornmeal biscuits and sweet corn cakes. Its wall of stone and brick stood in our way and forced the heat from the oven's red-hot coals and its choking smoke onto us.

How many more years would we have to keep on living with this black monster embedded in the house we lived in? Like an immovable rock it pushed us aside, shoved us all together and sucked in the very last breath of fresh air. Its enormous gaping mouth swallowed up my impatient question, incinerated it and reduced it to ashes, just as it did with the dry logs of *guachipelín* and black wood.

A thirst for vengeance made me dream of the happy day when we would demolish that monster and throw it out the door with its tongues of flame, its black smoke, and its acrid ashes—and our house would be clean, fresh, and bright.

Fantasies, nothing more than a poor girl's fantasies. That oven was what provided our daily sustenance, the money to buy my books, and this year also the money to pay for my graduation. The oven had to be roused to do more, so we could buy my white dress and new shoes and pay the fees for the diploma of a teacher, a graduate of the Institute.

"Nothing fancy," said my mother, holding to her policy of austerity and modesty.

"We'll have to put shoes on at least the two oldest children," protested Aunt Chana. "It would be a disgrace for them to go barefoot on that day."

"I'll make the shoes as a present. Put them down to my expense," promised Uncle Daniel.

"And I'll make a jug of eggnog," my grandmother offered, appearing at the kitchen door.

We were making plans and more plans every day, trying to solve the numerous problems that poor families have to deal with, from a baby-sitter for the youngest children to the outlay for new shoes and a new suit of cashmere for my father and for a dress for Aunt Chana and one for my mother.

The months went by and finally it was December.[1] Overflowing with pride and joy, I notified all our relatives that I had made it through my fifth year and was a schoolteacher and graduate of the Teachers Institute.

They were surprised and filled with admiration. I felt flattered by their asking me the details of my grades, about the prizes, and regarding preparations for graduation.

I felt as if I were on a throne, surrounded by admirers: I had won the great battle not only for myself, but for this working-class family that through me was beginning to become part of the world of culture.

"Look, we mustn't only think of the celebration and the clothes. We have to give thanks to God for what he has granted us," said my aunt Chana. And she reminded my mother that they had to pay what they had vowed to the Virgin of Help if I came out well in my studies.

"Well, of all the silly old fools," cried Uncle Daniel. "That girl won out because she's a real fighter, that's why. Don't mess things up with fairy tales about miracles or that drivel about promises. The girl and you are the ones that sweated your heads off."

---

[1]In Latin America, the school year generally runs from about March to December.

*

On December 17, 1922, six of my family were standing on the sidewalk in front of the Institute, waiting from before seven o'clock in the evening for the doors to open, so they could be first to enter the *Sala Magna*.

All looked very smart and were wearing brand-new shoes and clothes. I had never seen my mother looking like that before. She was wearing a lovely dress of blue crepe with silver-plated buttons. My aunt Chana, always fresh and pretty, and with her heavy black braids, wore a strawberry-colored dress with little insets of lace trimming. My father, with his striking features and his big mustache, looked most elegant wearing his new suit and red tie. Uncle Daniel, clean as a whistle, did not look like a vulgar-spoken, sharp-tongued shoemaker, but like a distinguished gentleman. The two children remained standing, like dolls, not daring to sit down in any seat.

With the genuine timidity and respectful attitude of the poor, my six family members looked for a place to sit together on the chairs in the section on the left. Surprised, they admired the elegance and solemnity of the *Sala Magna*, while they eagerly awaited the part of the program where I would appear in my white graduation dress and receive my teacher's diploma.

All of the boys and girls of our class were spending our last hours in the classroom in lively chatter with the open-hearted friendliness of naïve and happy young students. We believed that we would hold the world in our hands once we received our professional diplomas.

Wearing my new dress of fine white wool, trimmed with bands of lustrous white silk, I felt strange and nervous. I was biting my nails, while my cold hands and burning cheeks betrayed my intense emotion.

To the strains of the "March of Triumph" from *Aïda*, we students and teachers solemnly filed into the *Sala Magna*, crowded with children, relatives, and friends of the graduates. Warm applause greeted us as we seated ourselves in the first rows, which were specially reserved for us.

I eagerly looked for my folks and from far back they looked at me with pride and joy. I raised my hands way up high to let them know I was there and where I was seated in the big hall. The notes of the national hymn and the four-part chorus singing "Alma Mater" signaled the opening of the graduation exercises of the teachers of the Institute in that December of 1922.

The magical words of Don Omar, exhorting us to fulfill our mission as teachers and future builders of a new and great nation, inspired us, imbuing us with courage and hope for the work that we had to carry out as new teachers, graduates of the Teachers Training Institute of Costa Rica.

In the shadow of the national tricolor flag and the blue banner of the Institute, there lay on the stage the thirty diplomas to be handed out that memorable night. We were called in alphabetical order, one by one. As each one walked off the stage, the boys and girls went to their parents, gave them a kiss, and handed the diploma they had just received over to them. As for me, my strength failed me. I could not walk to the back of the hall, where my parents were. I had a lump in my throat and was unable to take a step. I went back to my fellow students with my diploma clutched very tightly in my sweaty palms.

At the exit, my mother and Aunt Chana, who were waiting for me on the sidewalk, snatched the diploma from me. My relatives surrounded them to admire that prize, which they now regarded as having been won by the whole family.

"Say, girl, what happened to you? Why didn't you come like the others and give the diploma to your mama?" asked my father, rather annoyed.

"Don't scold her, don't say a word. You know how shy that girl is. It is a miracle that she was able to get ahead, poor girl," said my mother, putting her blue scarf over my head to protect me from the cold December drizzle.

"Open your umbrellas! Watch out the diploma doesn't get wet! Don't let a spot get on it!" called my aunt Chana worriedly from under the rain, which was beginning to come down hard.

15. The Road of Life

That Monday, the 18th of December, 1922, dawned like a day that was new and different. Everybody at home was talking about the success of my graduation, the fiesta at the Institute, and the excitement they felt when they saw me go up the steps to the stage to receive my diploma. My grandmother, who could not go because she had to take care of the youngest children, gave me a present of a small sack of snow-white canvas containing little balls of camphor, so I could keep my diploma in it, safe from the rats and roaches.

And we all went back to the bustle and commotion of the regular workday. It was December, a magnificent month for earning extra money to help pay off the debts we had incurred for the expenses of my graduation.

Once again I took on my job at the bakery alongside my mother, while we were making new plans and beginning to imagine our family's future, this time with new economic and social goals.

"We must get out of this barrio," declared my mother. "With the nice little salary you're going to earn, we'll be able to rent a house with a wood floor."

It had always been our lot to live in houses with hard black floors of plain dirt. To leave this level and be able to live in a house with a wood floor meant climbing the social ladder a good few inches higher.

"You're quite right," put in my aunt Chana, "but following this luxury will come others. How are we going to live in a different and better house if we don't have even one piece of decent furniture? How will these benches and boxes look on a polished wood floor?"

"It doesn't matter," replied my mother. "We have to get away from this pigsty, no matter what. We'll manage things as we go.

Now she's going to make a good little salary, we can get some furniture on installments."

"Yes, yes, and we'll throw out those old beds, cots, and ripped-up sleeping mats that are just a disgrace," I added, imagining I had in my hands many thousands of colons, giving me immense power to completely change the economic circumstances in our home.

"Don't go crazy! Don't start building castles in the air," called my uncle Daniel from his shoemaker's bench. "Wait till you see some cash come in first. You think it's so easy to find a job? Just because you have a diploma, all doors are going to open for you? Don't be so silly!"

Uncle Daniel turned out to be right. In spite of my fine diploma as a teacher and as a Teachers Institute graduate with excellent grades, I had to wait six long months for the government to assign me a place in a school in Guadalupe in 1923.

Bewildered and disenchanted, I sought out a teacher friend of mine to tell him my tragedy, and he soothed my pain with this cheap advice:

"Your wings are not clipped as long as your thoughts are as free as the wind."

I never knew whether this vulgar philosophy was produced by his own brain or whether it came from some other author as mediocre as he was, but at that time it sounded just wonderful to me. For many years I saved it, copied into one of the little notebooks where I used to jot down the sayings of thinkers that impressed me in the years of my youth.

Some years later I realized that this nonentity was a simple philanthropic Rotarian. I tore the page out of my notebook and threw it in the garbage. It was like a kitschy color print and beclouded and deflected my thoughts.

16.   Teacher in Guadalupe: 1923

I began my work as teacher in the town of Guadalupe with the enterprising spirit of a Don Quixote, bringing with me the most advanced teaching plans and all the enthusiasm of a young teacher nineteen years of age.

My mother had made me a lovely red dress with pleats and a white collar. I wore it for the first time on this happy Monday in the month of August when at six-thirty in the morning I caught a yellow streetcar to Pilar Jiménez School, where I was to take charge of a fourth grade classroom of boys.

A good-looking and courteous director received me very kindly and gave me initial instructions for my work. Several older teachers, in their fifties but looking like pensioners, greeted me somewhat disdainfully and a brood of loud and sweaty boys got to their feet when the director introduced me.

I was left to face that group of boys of ten and eleven years of age all by myself. I felt deeply moved and at the same time bewildered in front of so many eyes and open mouths awaiting my teaching.

It was as though I were trying to loosen the string from a spool where I had carried my knowledge rolled up. I pulled at the string, timidly greeting my first pupils and trying to win them over before starting on the arithmetic lesson. I read them in oratorical style the story *"Meñique"* ["Pinkie"], by Martí, following with precision all the instructions given us by Carmen Lyra in her lectures on children's literature at the Teachers Institute.

"Read us another one, Miss, read us another," at the end shouted a chorus of all the children who had enjoyed with me the pure and beautiful prose of the great Cuban poet.

The bell rang for recess, and I went out with my pupils to play on the square while the tired old teachers whispered in the corridors of the school.

I heard how one of them said, when she saw me running about with the children, "New brooms sweep clean. She'll soon get over those newfangled notions."

When recess was over, one of the boys reminded me that I had not yet called the roll. It was true: there on the desk lay a white notebook, lined, with the names of my pupils. I turned it over to the same boy for him to note down those absent and those present. That was how I began putting into practice the new teaching methods which called for an individual approach to the pupil:

Eloy Retana, present.
Rafael Molina, present.
Francisco Castillo, present.
Arturo Gutiérrez, absent. "Sick. Got a nail in his heel," reported a boy.
Carlos Torres, absent. "His mama's in the hospital."
Luis García, present.
Marcos Monge, present.
Hugo Leitón, absent. "He went to live in Siquirres."
Elías Espinoza, present.
Otoniel Arguedas, absent. "Can't come back to school. Has to work," another boy reported.
Manuel Calderón, present.

Thus from the first day of school, the images of my thirty pupils were paraded before my eyes. They were boys of flesh and blood, most of them barefoot, practically all skinny and showing signs of malnutrition. Undisciplined, inattentive, and badly behaved, they were ready for fights and fisticuffs at the drop of a hat.

At ten o'clock in the morning, many of the boys began asking for permission to leave. They had to go to San José and bring lunch to their fathers, who were working there in factories or stores. There, under their desks, was where they kept the mesh shoulder bags in which they carried the lunches, wrapped in banana leaves.

This was the raw material I had to work with in order to put into practice my ideals and modern teaching methods.

I knew by heart the entire teaching process of the famous "centers of interest"—food, housing, clothing, transportation, etc., etc. I had earned brilliant grades making perfect projects with excellent illustrations in my notebook on methodology. But, oh Lord, now it was a different song.

Before me was the hard reality of the life these poor children led. Like my little cousins and my younger brothers and sisters, they matured prematurely and were crushed by the unfair limitations put on them in their lives as working-class children.

Every afternoon when I got home, I would recount my experiences of the day. My reports would provoke valuable political and social comments from the family members. Although they did not understand the economic phenomenon, they followed their class instincts in judging the reports I made there in the open storage shed, where the dough was warmed and the dozens of shirts were ironed that my grandmother had washed.

"These things can't be helped, girl," declared my aunt Chana, trying to explain the fate of the poor. "There have always been rich and poor, and there always will be till the end of the world. It says so in the Holy Bible."

"Don't be telling lies! Have you by any chance ever read the Bible? Don't invent such stupidities—you wouldn't even recognize the book by its cover," grumbled my uncle Daniel, cutting a piece of shoe leather on a board he held on his knees.

The fact was that not one member of the family, not even I myself, who was now regarded as a learned person, could explain these social phenomena.

The argument calmed down to a considerable degree when I announced that at the end of the month I would receive my first month's salary as a teacher—one hundred colons, ready cash.

Another row was in the making.

"Tell me one thing—is that girl going to hand over her whole pay to you or are you going to let her squander it herself just like that?" inquired my aunt.

"Don't be so overcritical," said my mother. "She's a very sensible girl, and I'm going to give her the pleasure of spending her first salary on whatever she wants. She certainly deserves it."

"Don't give her wings like that. I tell you these days it's dangerous to give free rein to girls. If it was my daughter, she would hear a song from a different rooster," Aunt Chana told my mother.

My mother kept her word, which I took as proof of her complete confidence in me.

When I cashed my first paycheck as teacher, I counted the money over and over again. It was a sum I had never seen in my hands before. I made a thousand plans and figured up and down. I made a very close guess and laid aside twenty-five colons as the additional price I would have to pay to rent a house somewhere far away from that barrio of La Puebla. With the remainder of the money, I bought two blankets for the littlest children, a flask of flower scented water for my grandmother, a bar of fragrant face soap for my aunt Chana, several pairs of socks for my father, and two pounds of Edam cheese for my mother, who had been wishing for that cheese for a long time. For Uncle Daniel I bought a pack of fine cigarettes, and for the youngsters I bought water whistles, balloons, and a jar of candies.

I got home loaded down like Santa Claus, as happy and euphoric as if I had won first prize in the lottery. There in the open shed, we had a grand fiesta with both big and small, celebrating this event without precedent in the history of our family.

17. From La Puebla to Barrio Mexico: 1924

Allow me to transform my spirit into my brick
schoolhouse. Let the flame of my enthusiasm enfold the
school's poor courtyard, its bare classroom. Let my heart
provide more support and my goodwill more gold than
the columns and the gold of the rich schools.
> — Gabriela Mistral, *"La Oración de la Maestra"*
> ["The Teacher's Prayer"]

I taught at the school in Guadalupe for two years, swimming
against the current with arms outstretched, trying to break routines
by the force of my enthusiasm and the freshness of my youth. These
gave me inexhaustible courage to try out the new pedagogic ideas
that I tried to introduce wherever there was the slightest possibility.

I could say that I accomplished miracles, going by the common
saying that faith moves mountains. The school's sordid, dried-up
atmosphere had to be transformed. The respect and sympathies of the
people of the town had to be won. It was necessary to bring culture
and a joyful spirit to these poor youngsters, who repeated the multiplication tables and the names of the rivers and cities of Costa Rica
like so many parrots. Schools like that had to be made attractive with
plants and flowers, music, and artistic pictures. Day and night I
dreamed of the great plans I had in mind to carry out at that rural

school,[1] a school that I would make modern, revolutionary, more humane, and more vital, in accord with the new scientific theories and the social advances in the world.

Poor little twenty-year old teacher! Naïve and poetic, I imagined that my school was like a secluded garden, encircled and ready to begin its efforts to experiment with poor children who came from a distance, very often hungry, ill, and bewildered by the problems besetting their families.

Lost and disturbed at the difference between the pedagogic theories and the problems at my school, I was unable to understand the inexplicable contradictions that barred the road to my fantastic plans.

Riding in the yellow streetcar that brought me every morning from Central Street in San José to Guadalupe Plaza, I could see the humble homes of my pupils, who were running in haste trying to win a race with the streetcar. Their little bare feet left moist footprints on the street pavements, and their steps fell like heavy weights on my teacher's heart.

"All these children have to be given shoes," I said boldly to myself, as if I had thousands of shoes on hand for them. "Dining rooms have to be put into all the schools. A children's theater must be organized. Playgrounds need to be opened up in all the barrios. Small traveling libraries have to be organized for all the people in the barrios. We need to establish choruses and children's orchestras. Laboratories and workshops ought to be equipped and set up in all the schools and academies. Athletic fields....we must...."

The streetcar conductor rang the bell hard to let us know we had reached Guadalupe Plaza. My pupils were waiting for me there, very well behaved on this day, because the school inspector had arrived very early to conduct the year-end final examinations.

Along with the thousand projects that I had for my school, I also dreamed of transforming the living conditions of my family. My

---

[1]No longer rural, the neighborhood is now a crowded working-class barrio. Nearby is the large open air farmers' market, where thousands of shoppers buy food every weekend.

feet kept refusing to go on passing along those streets in La Puebla barrio. And at times I felt afraid that my pupils might learn that their teacher lived in such a horrible, indecent, and unfriendly barrio.

With indescribable zeal, I hastened to try to get out of that pigsty, as my aunt Chana called it. Every afternoon after work, I went through the barrios of San José, looking for a house that was clean, decent, and cheap, one that I could afford to rent with my new salary as teacher.

To search for a house among the thousands and thousands of houses in the capital was a thankless task. To go through the barrios from top to bottom, from here to there, until darkness fell, to haggle over prices and compare conditions was a Way of the Cross, endlessly long and humiliating, arousing my protests against harsh landlords and profiteers.

I sprang from one sidewalk to the other when I saw a "For Rent" sign pasted onto a large, sparkling clean window. Or I would hasten toward another house, surrounded by a garden, and with handsome wrought-iron gratings, that had been standing vacant many months. But the miracle failed to happen, for reality was implacable, and my calculations and aspirations belonged in the realm of fantasy.

"I don't know what that girl is after. It looks to me like her airs and conceits are going to her brain. If it was up to her, she'd have us go and live next door to the Presidential Palace or the Cathedral," said Aunt Chana, critical of my aspirations.

"It's not that she's taken leave of her senses. The thing is that she's not like us. We're just work animals. We'll throw ourselves down to sleep on any old sleeping mat. We'll eat at the edge of the hearth in the midst of the smoke and ashes. That's how it is...."

"Yes, that's the big deal now. What a lot of foolishness! I can see the demands and luxuries coming. One of these days she'll probably even be ashamed to say that I'm her uncle," said Daniel, prophesying a possible flight from my social class.

"I'm not going back on my family nor on my own kind, but for sure I'm sick and tired of living in this horrible barrio. I want to leave it together with all of you, even if you don't care about leaving.

I'm going, and I don't care how much it costs. I don't want to live in this filthy, awful neighborhood any more!" I shouted in desperation.

"That girl has turned out to be very badly behaved, very insolent, and we're going to get it in the neck from her," said my aunt, very worried.

With tenacious, aggressive obstinacy, I searched on tirelessly for my right to live in a clean, light house, far from the districts of the south. Then I turned toward the north of the city, along the Cow Pass, until I got to Mexico barrio. There at last I found a clean, modest little house for fifty colons a month rent, on 11th Avenue between 14th and 16th Streets.

I carried my intention through. Without consulting anyone, I paid the first month's rent in advance as soon as I got my pay for April, 1924.

I arrived home with the rent receipt in my hand and immediately announced my decision, like an order that could not be postponed. It fell on the family like a bombshell.

"Child of God!" cried my mother, greatly alarmed. "Did you check to see if there is enough room for the oven?"

"Of course I did! There's a big yard in back. We can put up a big shed to hold that mastodon," I told her. I knew that we would still have to put up with that black, smoky monster for many years to come.

Moving from such a slum to a middle-class barrio was a great event. It was a decisive change that would influence the psychology, the morals, and the philosophy of the entire family. We were going to enter a new social environment, with new neighbors, new surroundings, a new vocabulary, new gestures, and new standards of living, based on the new situation, although always still within the difficult conditions of artisan labor.

It seemed as if we were going abroad, to judge by the preparations for moving, which we all excitedly started on that very evening.

"The best thing would be for us to go there between darkness and dawn and get there, say, at half past five in the morning," said Aunt Chana, concerned about moving so much ugly old junk that would embarrass us before the neighbors in Mexico barrio.

"What can we do, girl? We're working people; we're poor but honest. We can't pretend to be what we're not," was my mother's reply to my aunt's fears.

And so we all began a great hustle and bustle, packing our belongings, such as they were, into boxes and baskets and making bundles of every size, which we would load into the two carts we had rented for the next day at six in the morning.

The confusion and noise that night was like a fiesta and indescribably exciting, above all for the children. They enjoyed the spectacle and helped to find things and pack up all kinds of tools. They fixed up a place to sleep on the floor for this night, since the beds were already taken apart.

At six-thirty sharp on Saturday morning, we began to load our junk into the carts, before the curious eyes of our neighbors, who, intrigued, asked where we were moving.

"To Mexico barrio!" I told them. "To find a better life! To breathe fresh air!"

The children scrambled up to the top of the load on both of the carts and showed off there as if they were seated in the imperial carriage. My father walked along in front, watching over everything and guiding the owner of the carts to 14th Street and 11th Avenue.

I went ahead, carrying the door key, and entered the house first. Then I waited at the door like an owner and lady of the house in this great adventure.

My uncle Daniel stubbornly remained in the big shed, where the oven was and where he had his worktable. He was angry and did not want to go to live with us in Mexico barrio.

"You go ahead. I'm staying and living here in this barrio. Here's where I have my workshop and my customers," he said, gathering up his metal work tools and putting them into a mesh bag.

"The people in that barrio are a bunch of stuffed shirts...you'll soon find out," he said in a disdainful tone and with a certain nostalgia, kicking some old pots around that we had thrown out in the backyard.

18. From the School in Guadalupe to the Preschool: 1925

I was beginning to put roots down in Pilar Jiménez School in Guadalupe when, one evening, my great friend Carmen Lyra came over to the house and asked me to work with her to establish a new Montessori preschool.[1] Carmen Lyra had been thinking about this project since her return from Europe, where she had studied modern methods in preschool education.

Such an honor and mark of distinction from my dear professor left me both astonished and frightened, for I was afraid of losing the experience and security of my place in the Guadalupe school. At the same time, however, I felt proud and happy that the noted writer had thought of me when considering teachers for her school.

"Mama, Mama, here comes Miss Isabel. Come and say hello to her," I called from the front door.

"I'm coming, girl. Wait till I change my apron," answered my mother, all aflutter at having a visitor of such high rank. Wiping the sweat off with her clean apron, she excitedly greeted my professor, a woman modest and humane like no other. The two of them had a long talk, as if they had been old friends, and then the three of us

---

[1]Maria Montessori (1870-1952), Italian educator who created a system for training and teaching young children which emphasizes self-learning and training of the senses.

together decided I would accept the offer to go to work at the new preschool.

"What a delicious smell!" said Carmen Lyra, sniffing with her broad nose, trying to make the family members feel comfortable with her. They had left their work to come and take a look and see what this professor was like whom I had told them so much about. The mouth-watering aroma of the cornmeal biscuits in the oven pervaded the whole house and aroused Carmen Lyra's appetite and her mischievous curiosity.

"Invite her to have some corn rings and coffee," said Aunt Chana, always forward and unceremonious.

"Do you think she'll like such ordinary biscuits?" asked my mother doubtfully, trying to imagine the refined tastes of a professor.

"Of course, señora, definitely. I'm a big glutton. I'm a regular Indian when it comes to something like biscuits made of corn," replied Carmen Lyra, thanking my aunt Chana for her invitation.

I didn't know what to do in this predicament, which filled me with embarrassment and concern, because I had to take the professor to the kitchen itself. There we had no proper chairs, only rough benches and a table with a faded old covering. But everything worked out like a thousand miracles. Carmen Lyra, with her exquisite tact and her natural human sensitivity, made it a warm and happy party, winning the sympathies and confidence of the folks in the house. They were surprised to see her eating with such enjoyment as she used her fingers to lift out the puffed-up cornmeal rings she had dunked in her cup of hot black coffee.

When she was leaving, my mother gave her a little bag of the corn rings, which Carmen Lyra said would not last her for even a day.

"Go along with her," ordered my mother.

And I, happy with such encouragement, went that evening along North Seventh Avenue, walking east toward Carmen Lyra's, where purple *guarias*[2] were already blooming on the adobe wall of that unforgettable little house.

---

[2]An indigenous orchid.

*

It was the month of February. Carmen Lyra and I were working together on the exciting task of preparing bold, modern plans to get the new preschool launched. The school would be placed at the service of slum children from the Torres River flats, from near Cow Pass, from the vicinity of the penitentiary, and from the hill at Five Corners.

We were full of enthusiasm and joy when one morning in April, 1926, we opened the doors of the preschool (behind the Metallic Building) to about a hundred children. They had come to be educated and to enjoy the special modern equipment in a sheltering environment. All was particularly prepared to try to cultivate the intellect and sensibilities of children from four to six years of age.

We watched them arrive all cleaned up and combed, held by the hands of their mothers or their aunts or little older sisters, who were going to leave them alone for the first time in such a modern preschool.

My heart of an idealistic young teacher was palpitating with happiness and enthusiasm—at last I would realize my dreams, my utopian pedagogy.

There were flowers everywhere that morning. There were toys, swings and seesaws, balls and dolls, lovely artistic pictures, and colored murals illustrating fairy tales and fables. The beautiful and kindly music teacher, Margarita Castro, played on the piano some charming children's rounds, graceful and poetic, written by Carmen Lyra.

The preschool was an oasis of peace, of joy, and of culture. I felt certain that out of this pedagogic garden would come happy, good children, for we had in our hands the scientific methods that we had learned from the books by Maria Montessori, Decroly,[3] and many other modern pedagogues.

---

[3] Ovid Decroly (1871-1932), Belgian pioneer in the education of young children.

Such methods could not fail—we were thoroughly grounded in the principles of psychology, so that we could establish habits of hygiene, discipline, study, and work in the children. We knew how to stimulate their artistic sensibilities and were convinced of the value of esthetic education, beginning with the earliest years of life.

We avidly read books and brochures on mental health, psychology, and anthropology to provide the basis for our plans and teaching methods.

Everything seemed to be going marvelously on the magical wheels of that pedagogic vehicle that we had set in motion in this vale of tears.

Every month we recorded the heights and weights of the children, according to their dates of birth, the data on the development of each child being calculated in complicated formulas. A graduate nurse regularly reviewed the data and noted the sad reality. Poor Ernesto, the son of Rita, the lottery ticket vendor, had barely sixty percent of the normal hemoglobin level. Angelilla, daughter of the laundress, had chronic rickets, hence her curved and deformed legs. Then there was Luisillo, always suffering from boils. And there was a little hunchbacked boy, full of mucus, and with a cough like a barking dog, interrupting the minutes of silence that we had in the program each morning to teach the children to listen attentively to passages of classical music.

The statistical data on the heights and weights recorded each month produced alarming figures. These did not fit into the indices for normal growth and development in children.

The human materials that arrived at the preschool were poor, sickly little plants, prematurely exhausted by the harsh, cold wind that blew implacably over so many innocent lives of hungry and malnourished children.

Theories of mental health went astray over the little heads with their dry skin, rough and dirty, or they got entangled among the small bare feet—those theories and philosophical concepts of education and the role of the school in society.

How could you set these children to dancing to the rhythms of music by Chopin, Handel, or Debussy?

How could you draw gracious steps and delicate movements from their little bodies, so that they might suggest blue dragonflies, droplets of water, or bright little stars?

A bitter smile appeared on Carmen Lyra's lips one day when she could bear it no longer and ordered the piano to be closed upon seeing the ridiculous, grotesque pirouettes that poor Angelilla made, trying to adapt her steps to the rhythm of the music of Chopin.

What vivid and cruel lessons life gave us every day in that preschool, at the side of Carmen Lyra, who would make us understand the contradictions between idealistic pedagogy and the realities that obstinately tore our plans and dreams to shreds.

"My little ones," said Carmen Lyra, "you should sleep with your windows open so you can breathe fresh air during the night." And poor Carlillos, who lived in Dagger Stab Alley, raised his small hand to ask a question.

"What should we do, Miss? My house doesn't have any windows." The poor child lived in a shack made of tin and old cardboard.

And poor Margarita, pale and with circles under her eyes? She always fell asleep in the music lessons. What a lazy and fretful little girl! She was always off somewhere on the moon. One day we happened to learn from a woman neighbor that the poor child was the daughter of a prostitute. Margarita had to wait for long hours, sitting in the front doorway while the mother attended to her customers.

How could we tell stories about fairies, elves, golden butterflies, or princes to that little girl living in Tin Plate barrio and that little black boy living in Nothing-is-worse?

How could we ask the mothers to cooperate with us when many of them begged us not to teach their children habits of hygiene, such as to brush their teeth or sleep in pajamas? These were impossible luxuries, beyond the reach of slum children who had trouble enough getting beans and rice to eat.

How could we speak of the Rights of the Child at the Congress of Educators being held at the National Theater, when at our very doors a brood of beggar children and shoeshine boys confronted us with their own reality?

Once more as before, pessimism and hopelessness enveloped my heart and disturbed my thoughts. I could find no explanation for the social problems that I saw every day in my school, in the streets of the city, and in the slum barrios of the capital. I felt myself to be in a maze, in an alley with no way out, seeing only "the hole in the doughnut."

Eminent sociologists, hygienists, pediatricians, educators, writers, national politicians, and foreigners discussed the issue in the press and gave conferences on the grave problems affecting national education, on the increase in the numbers of prostitutes, about the malnutrition of the people, etc., etc. Not one of these leading personalities dared to put a finger on the ulcer itself. Only Carmen Lyra, with her biting irony, raised blisters among the circles of intellectuals and politicians, who wrinkled their noses at the denunciations from her teacher's pen.

I followed these discussions and statements with passion, trying to find an explanation which would resolve my doubts and confusion.

I began to believe wholeheartedly in those slogans set forth by José Vasconcelos[4] and many other indigenous Latin American thinkers, who made such phrases fashionable as "The spirit will speak for my race" and "Forward to justice, for culture and liberty."

The beautiful and resounding slogans clearly pointed in the same direction as my aspirations.

"Yes, yes," I said to myself, "there's the key to the problem. First of all, people have to become educated, so they can learn to use liberty and understand justice and how to use it without abuses or resorting to violence. People have to be taught the doctrines of love, of forgiveness, of overcoming, so they will know how to make good use of the laws, fraternizing with all Costa Ricans, without making social distinctions. All of us teachers, like spiritual guides, are being called upon to carry out this great mission on earth."

---

[4]José Vasconcelos (1882-1959), Mexican educator, politician, philosopher and writer. As Minister of Education (1920-1924), he initiated an ambitious program of mass education, especially in rural areas.

The brilliant arguments made by Omar Dengo concerning the problems of culture and the development of the human personality continued to passionately drive my criteria of an idealistic teacher, believing as I did that I held in my hands the miraculous gift of being able to form the souls and even help change the fate of all the children that attended my school.

I put quotation marks around the vibrant and beautiful sentences that the great Omar Dengo had spoken in his lectures in the Institute. They inspired me, and I adjusted my thoughts to follow his philosophy to the letter:

> "To redeem man from misery without redeeming him from passion, vice, and ignorance is not a serious solution to any problem."

"It's true. it's true," I thought. "First, the soul has to be purified. That's the main thing, the soul."

> "The deepest evil, the profound evil where the human tragedy is forged, is not rooted in the difference between rich and poor, but in what becomes firmly established in the attitude of the spirit, which, to me, is determined by cosmic designs unknown to us."

Cosmic designs, unknown.... What could that mean? Can it be that the stars from way up there direct the fortunes and destinies of us human beings who live in this world? Could it be that this was the true explanation? I asked myself, recalling the naïve and picturesque interpretations that my aunt Chana offered every time when discussions came up about the good fortune or injustice met by some relative or friend. It always seemed to be hanging by a thread from above, something mysterious, invisible, that swung them from here to there, causing jumps and leaps unforeseen in this world.

"That Mr. so-and-so who always managed to land on his feet, regardless of which government was in power, was born in 1910, the year when Halley's comet appeared," said my aunt. She assured me as authoritatively as ever that those born at that time were very lucky people. On the other hand, that poor old crippled woman, who was born on a Tuesday the thirteenth,[5] has had to drag her miserable fate around with her like a millstone for having been born on such an unfortunate day.

Would I have to study astrology in order to find the explanation for so many doubts and uncertainties that arose in my mind, considering the complex social and economic problems we were seeing at the preschool?

Keeping my ignorance to myself, I searched in an encyclopedia for the exact definition of the word "cosmic," to try and understand what my beloved and respected professor was really saying, for his words had been the vibrant gospel that had inspired my soul. But this time it did not turn out that way: the tangle surrounding my mind like a prison was getting worse all the time, for according to the professor the problems were still more complicated and mysterious.

They could not be looked at with the simple criteria of a village priest, which is what people told me I was doing. People said that I was only a poor little schoolteacher with no comprehension of philosophy, unable to rise up any higher than the rooftop of my school. They said it was necessary for me to reach to the stars and not just exist at ground level, where I was so close to those little daily problems that I was no longer able to see the forest in all its grandeur and splendor.

Like a *matapalo*,[6] skepticism and despair began to wrap themselves around the preschool. Our work was like putting patches here and there on old threadbare cloth. It was like pouring water into a basket, as Carmen Lyra said.

---

[5]In Latin America, Tuesday the thirteenth is considered to be an unlucky day.

[6]Vernacular name for any of numerous chiefly tropical trees, shrubs, and vines belonging to the genus *Ficus*. The author is referring to a variety which often coils around other trees, eventually strangling its support (personal interview with Luisa González, May 6, 1993).

The generosity and kindness of our philanthropist friends could never be enough to solve so many problems—yes, those of daily life, like the basic necessities of a cup of coffee each morning with a bread roll, even if without butter or cheese; like having something to wear, and even to have a pair of shoes to be able to go to work, to high school, or to elementary school; to be able to pay the rent, even though the place is nothing but a filthy pigsty. Such are the small problems—bitter and difficult problems of every day, of every hour, of every minute, that like painful glass splinters pierce body and soul in millions of human beings who are suffering and dying in this world. Yes, here in this world, on this earth, so far from the bright planets that shine down on so much poverty and misery.

We could not escape the problems, but neither were we obligated to be like fossils and adopt the ridiculous, facile routine of the official teaching establishment in order to quietly accumulate the number of years needed to make sure of a good pension.

An acid ferment was corroding our beings, taking away all the joy and enthusiasm of our educational efforts, now so hopeless in outlook and so incompatible with the social situation.

We recognized the failure of our plans, but could not discover the reasons causing the problems these poor children in the preschool were suffering from.

We struggled on hopelessly every day in that sea of contradictions, feeling ourselves completely incapable of finding any basic solution to the grave economic and social problems confronting us.

What could we do about the poor watchman who lost his job and was left with no wages to support his seven children?

How could we help solve the problems of that poor widow who had to support her four small children all by herself?

How could we help poor Rita, who was evicted yesterday because she was unable to pay the twenty-five colons rent for that miserable little room?

Where could we get the money to buy the medications that Juanita, the laundress, needed for treatment of her rheumatism, which was making her almost an invalid?

How could one help shuddering at the sight of the scalded little arms of the toddler who was left alone in the house and pulled on a pot of boiling water?

"To the devil with pedagogy! Send this caricature, this farce of an education to blazes!" cried Carmen Lyra, seeing all our good intentions break like bubbles on the tragic reality that the poor children of the preschool lived through every day. She broke the crystal of her poetic and romantic lyricism. As if she were writing with an incandescent pen, she produced masterly reports, like etchings, depicting the rawest and cruelest scenes from the lives of these children and their mothers, with their homes being destroyed by ignorance and misery.

With a fine feeling for irony and critique, she placed in evidence the fantasies and farcical comedies being played out by the teaching establishment. A thousand times she ridiculed the "hypothetical child" that many deluded teachers living in the clouds invent. These teachers are hoping that culture alone, on its own, will produce the miracle of putting an end to the blackest of all crimes in this world—the starvation and exploitation of children.

19. Back Again to La Puebla Barrio: 1927-1932

> People are not revolutionaries because of animosity,
> but through the need for abundance.
>
> — Roger Garaudy[1]

> From the horizon of one to the horizon of all.
>
> — P. Éluard[2]

At that time, Carmen Lyra was the highest antenna vibrating in permanent tension and receiving the revolutionary waves which were bringing us messages of protest, of struggle, and of hope from the new world that was surging forth there in the land of Lenin.

Her generous hands and wide-awake mind were ready to help all the persecuted political persons who, on arrival in our country, came looking for the door to that small house on North Seventh Avenue. It was always open and hospitable toward these young Latin American students, who carried in their fists the torch of the anti-

---

[1]Roger Garaudy (b. 1913), French Marxist philosopher.

[2]Paul Éluard, (1895-1952), pen name of Eugène Grindel, French Communist poet.

imperialist struggle and their repudiation of the dictatorships of the Continent.

Carmen Lyra, the tiny but audacious teacher, was the one who, on that 13th of June, 1918, headed the civic march that ended with the burning of the newspaper *La Información* in protest against the dictatorship of the Tinocos. Without the slightest hesitation, she opened the doors of the preschool wide to all the revolutionaries and, under her charge, put the typewriters and mimeograph machines at their service. Along with these came her wisdom and her faithful support of the noble causes being defended by these young men from Venezuela, Peru, Central America....

At the preschool, we listened to these intelligent and courageous young fellows, their voices fired with passion. They had not five centimos in their pockets but carried handfuls of manifestos and messages to flood the Continent with their protests against the military dictatorships, the oligarchies and their Yankee accomplices who humiliate the people of Latin America.

A few of these youths did bow down and betray their ideals. Many others, the best, stood firm and became the yeast and fertilizer of the anti-imperialist struggles that broke out all over Latin America.

Those were the days of the Peruvian González Prada,[3] whose slogan "the old to the tomb and the youth to work" inflamed many young men and impelled them to take action; they were the years of the heroic struggle of Sandino;[4] the tragic years of the massacre of twenty thousand peasants in El Salvador;[5] years of the Marxist

---

[3]Manuel González Prada (1848-1918), poet, philosopher, and social critic. Founder of the Unión Nacional (National Union).

[4]Augusto César Sandino (1893-1934), Nicaraguan guerrilla war leader 1926-1933 who ended the twenty-year U.S. occupation of Nicaragua. Sandino's later followers, the Sandinistas, struggled eighteen years to overthrow the U.S.-installed Somoza dictatorship and won in 1979.

[5]In 1931, when reformist Arturo Araujo was elected president of El Salvador, the military quickly overthrew him. Peasant organizer Farabundo

initiatives of the Peruvian José Carlos Mariátegui;[6] the years of the heroic sacrifice of Sacco and Vanzetti; the years of the great pamphlet writers in Venezuela against the dictatorship of Juan Vicente Gómez;[7] the shining years of the great Soviet Revolution, whose advance has illuminated and astounded the entire world; the magnificent years of the *Repertorio Americano*, published by the great master García Monge, spokesman for progressive circles in Latin America; years of the Civic League, whose members included such eminent citizens as Dr. Ricardo Moreno Cañas,[8] Omar Dengo, Don Víctor Guardia, Dr. Julio César Ovares, Adriano Urbina, Víctor Quesada—all pioneers of the anti-imperialist struggles in Costa Rica.

The revolutionary impetus of the young people, who discussed with us the political and economic problems of their countries in relation to all their social problems, served to widen our horizons. We began to understand better where the roots lay of all the contradictions that troubled us and threw shadows of pessimism over our minds. These youngsters kindled in us a hatred against the bloody dictator of Venezuela, Juan Vicente Gómez; on sheets of paper, they

---

Martí led a revolt in January, 1932. The army swiftly crushed the uprising, systematically massacring 10,000 to 30,000 peasants. This atrocity, still known as *"la matanza"* ("the massacre"), marked the consolidation of political power by the Salvadoran military.

[6]Characterized by Frederick B. Pike (*The Modern History of Peru* [New York, N.Y.: Frederick A. Praeger, Inc., 1967]) as "perhaps the most original twentieth-century Peruvian intellectual," Mariátegui (1895-1930) was a founder of Peru's first Communist Party. He was a strong proponent that socialism must necessarily be connected with *indigenismo*, a movement which held up the descendants of the Incas living in the Andes and their traditional way of life as key to Peru's regeneration.

[7]Juan Vicente Gómez (1859-1935) seized power in 1908 and was dictator until 1935.

[8]Dr. Ricardo Moreno Cañas (1890-1938), physician and political leader, Director of Surgery at the San Juan de Diós Hospital in San José. Elected deputy in the National Legislature in 1932, he opposed concessions to foreign companies, especially United Fruit (Creedman, 1977).

hotly denounced to the world the horrors of the tortures and persecutions being inflicted on the political prisoners in the jails of the tyrants of Chile, Peru, Paraguay, and Nicaragua.

Even on Sundays, the typewriters and mimeograph machines went on working. The preschool had become more of a mother than ever, since it was widening our horizons to as far away as the Andes and the land of Bolívar and serving as a bridge to get revolutionary messages and protests through to all the nations of the Continent.

We were beginning to glean here and there among so many political and social theories, when one morning we found the newspaper *Revolución*[9] pushed under the door of the main entrance to the preschool. It was a small printed sheet folded in half. It had been slipped there by the revolutionary carpenter Gonzalo Montero Berry, an intelligent and educated worker, one of the founders of the Communist Party of Costa Rica. It was the first red newspaper put out by the young Communists, bold and courageous law students who were the first to raise the banner of the hammer and sickle in Costa Rica.

Carmen Lyra picked it up with great curiosity and put it away in the notebooks she kept as director of the preschool. I wanted to get a copy of that tiny publication, the name of which aroused my curiosity, but she took no notice of my interest and carried it home with her, as with so many other publications that came to the office of the preschool.

On an afternoon of the following week, Carmen Lyra invited me to read a small booklet in French which she was translating and commenting on with me. "From what the boys say," she told me, "it's essential to study this pamphlet to be able to understand what's going on in the world."

There, sitting in the children's little chairs, we began to read that thin pamphlet of fifty pages, so insignificant looking from the outside: it was the *Communist Manifesto*, by Marx and Engels.

---

[9]A newspaper published by a group of law students led by Manuel Mora Valverde. It was issued for about a year from March 15, 1930 (Creedman, 1977).

"A specter is haunting Europe—the specter of
Communism."

"The history of all hitherto existing society is the history
of class struggles."

During the course of several evenings, we read these pages
again and again. Then we got directly in touch with those young
revolutionary Costa Ricans, who explained to us with clear understanding the materialist philosophy contained in that historic docu-
ment, which signaled the opening of a new era for all the people of
the world.

After that we were able to place our school's problems within
the framework of the total social and economic phenomenon of the
class struggle. It became clear that education is not a problem isolated from society's economic and political phenomena; nor can it be
solved through utopian, idealistic plans separate from the social
regime under which the school is operating.

Neither the teaching methods employed nor whether the theories were more advanced or less advanced were decisive. Basic was
the fact that the foundations of our school were laid upon shifting
sands in which there was no way that our dreams, our ideals of
spiritual teachers could take root.

And we decided to take the road of the left.

One night we went to Rescia Hall, located in front of Porfirio
Brenes School, to see the meetings of the workers and hear the
speeches of Manuel Mora,[10] Jaime Cerdas,[11] Luis Carballo, and
Adolfo Braña.

---

[10]Manuel Mora Valverde (b.1910), one of the principal founders of the
Communist Party of Costa Rica, which he headed until 1983. Author of
numerous political works and brochures. Deputy in the National Legislature
in 1934-1948 and 1970-1974. Candidate for the presidency of Costa Rica
1970 and 1974 (Creedman, 1977).

[11]One of the founders of the Communist Party of Costa Rica, Jaime Cerdas
Mora (b.1904) was a leader in the 1934 banana strike and served as a
deputy in the National Legislature in 1946-1948 (Creedman, 1977).

There were the sweaty workers sitting on rough wooden benches, many standing and others squatting; mouthfuls of warm air and cigarette smoke pervaded the atmosphere of that small hall, where a red flag shone triumphantly under a large portrait of Lenin. Children, women, and men passionately applauded the speeches of the young leaders, who presented the grave problems of worker unemployment, hunger among the people, the economic crisis, and persecution by employers. At the same time, they praised the great triumphs of the Soviet Revolution as an example of the world revolutionary movement, as an example of power in the hands of the working class, and as the only way to put an end to the exploitation of man by man.

Their fists raised high, they sang the *"Internationale,"* their tone aggressive and their voices rumbling deep in their throats:

> "Arise, you prisoners of starvation!
> Arise, you wretched of the earth!...."

> "'Tis the final conflict;
> Let each stand in his place...."

A strange shiver went through me from head to foot. I seemed to be living in the glorious days of the French Revolution. It was impossible to distance oneself from this atmosphere, impossible to be just a spectator. We too raised our fists high together with the workers, and we decided from that night on to dedicate ourselves to the revolutionary struggle and take the "only road," the road of social revolution.

I asked an old man who was standing next to me if he would copy that song down, and he told me:

"I don't know how to write, señora, but I could sing it for you, and you could write it down."

We moved over to a window. He sang the verses to me in a low voice a couple of times while I copied the words into a small notebook:

"Arise, you prisoners of starvation!
Arise, you wretched of the earth!"

I compared that verse with Martí's poem:

"With the poor of this earth
I want to share my fate."

And in indestructible union, I joined myself and my fate forever to the party of the working class, the party of my people.

Once more I returned, to go back and forth over those streets in La Puebla for many nights and many days, in that same barrio of my childhood, along the same block where I lived through my adventures as a poor youngster. I seemed to see the small footprints of my feet on the sidewalks of the barrio. I seemed to see the black and smoking flatiron. I imagined I heard my mother and my aunt Chana calling me from the sidewalk in front of that forever crumbling, ugly house.

I passed by that very door and, in a gesture of defiance, I pulled out the card of the Party, of my Party, that made me "see the splendor of the world and the possibility of joy." I wanted to nail my card on that door as a challenge, to show it to the neighbors of this barrio, and to take them all along with me to Rescia Hall.

I turned the corner at Porfirio Brenes School, going east, and with a firm, sure step full of joy and hope, I presented myself punctually at seven in the evening to fulfill the first task that my Party had entrusted me with—to give a basic course in geography to a small group of workers. Over a map of the world, yellowed and torn, nailed to the wall, my teacher's hands joined with the hard hands of bricklayers, shoemakers, and carpenters eagerly looking for that faroff land that was kindling dreams and hopes in their strong, sweaty faces.

Retired physician Regina Pustan has had the great good fortune in her life to attend medical school in the Soviet Union and the German Democratic Republic; to take part in the San Francisco to Moscow Walk for Peace in 1961-62; to join demonstrations against the Vietnam War; to volunteer in Central America; to discover the twin prizewinning gems of literature of Luisa González — her autobiography and her full-length play; and to find good friends to bring them before the U.S.A. public.

Robert French received his doctoral degree in social anthropology from Harvard University. He is the director of United Front Child Development Programs, a community-based agency serving low-income children and families in New Bedford, Massachusetts. He is involved in children's, community, labor, and foreign policy issues.

Maria Ogalde Gallardo was born in the village of Illapel, Chile, but was forced into exile with her family following the 1973 military coup. She attended the University of Chile and Roger Williams College, where she received her bachelor's degree in early childhood education. She is a teacher and activist in the struggle to help children.